Losing Control

Popular Politics & Governance In America

Steven E. Schier
General Editor

Vol. 8

PETER LANG
New York • Washington, D.C./Baltimore • Bern
Frankfurt am Main • Berlin • Brussels • Vienna • Oxford

Arthur Sanders

Losing Control

Presidential Elections and the Decline of Democracy

PETER LANG
New York • Washington, D.C./Baltimore • Bern
Frankfurt am Main • Berlin • Brussels • Vienna • Oxford

Library of Congress Cataloging-in-Publication Data

Sanders, Arthur B.
Losing control: presidential elections and the decline of democracy /
Arthur Sanders.
p. cm. — (Popular politics and governance in America; v. 8)
Includes bibliographical references and index.
1. Presidents—United States—Election. 2. Political participation—
United States. 3. Apathy—United States. 4. Democracy—United States.
I. Title. II. Series.
JK528 .S25 324.973'0931—dc22 2006100459
ISBN 978-0-8204-6722-1
ISSN 1529-241X

Bibliographic information published by **Die Deutsche Bibliothek**.
Die Deutsche Bibliothek lists this publication in the "Deutsche Nationalbibliografie"; detailed bibliographic data is available on the Internet at http://dnb.ddb.de/.

Cover image by Deborah Pappenheimer

29 Broadway, 18th floor, New York, NY 10006
www.peterlang.com

As always,
for Deb and for Ben.

TABLE OF CONTENTS

TABLES

FOREWORD

The book benefits from the help and guidance of many people. Steven Schier, who was the series editor for Peter Lang, encouraged me to write this book and provided good advice on an early outline of its contents. The material also draws upon research that I did in collaboration with many others as part of a project focused on money, parties, groups and elections organized by David Magleby at the Center for the Study of Elections and Democracy at Brigham Young University. I worked on case studies for that project with David Redlawsk of the University of Iowa in 2000 and 2002, and on my own in 2004. The papers, monographs, articles and chapters that have been produced for this project involved collaborative research of the most rewarding kind. The conversations we had when we met to discuss or present our work were always lively and informative. I learned an enormous amount about the election process generally and the Presidential election process specifically through my participation in these activities. I owe a special debt to David Magleby, Quin Monson and Kelley Patterson, who coordinated these projects and studies, and to David Redlawsk, my co-author on two of my case studies, but my debt is to all who were involved in the many panels, conferences and presentations over the years. I dare not list them all by name for fear that I will forget and therefore slight someone. But to all involved in the CSED projects, a sincere thanks. And a thanks as well to all the students who helped me in my research on these projects (too numerous to name), collecting materials for me, observing the Iowa caucuses and reporting back what they saw, and to my research assistants, Laura Clayton, Nicole Cooper, and Brian Wold, who helped compile all of the data from a variety of sources.

I also owe thanks to my colleagues here at Drake University. Our conversations over the years about how we elect our Presidents have always been both enjoyable and informative. Special thanks, in that regard, to Dennis Goldford, Rachel Caufield, David Skidmore, Deb DeLaet, Eleanor Zeff and, our former colleague, John Haskell.

Some of the data that is presented from the American National Election Studies were made available by the Interuniversity Consortium for Political and Social Research. Neither the original collectors of the data nor the consortium bears any responsibility for the analyses and interpretations presented here.

The students in my American Electoral Process, Media and Modern Politics, Public Opinion and Comparative Political Parties and Interest Groups classes over the years have also provided me with a stimulating environment within which to discuss these ideas. Those classes and this book are a testament to the synergy that exists between teaching and research.

Drake University has been a supportive environment as well. My sabbatical leave in the 2003 - 2004 year provided me with time to gather much data and begin writing the manuscript. Drake also provided a forum where I could begin to sketch out my conclusions at the annual Stalnaker Lecture in 2005. The feedback I received, both at the lecture and subsequently, was extremely helpful.

Everyone I have had to work with at Peter Lang Publishing, particularly Phyllis Korper and Sophie Appel, have been both responsive and helpful.

And finally, I want to thank my family. My wife and son, Deborah and Ben Pappenheimer, are an endless source of love, support and understanding. The richness and joy that I have in my life flows from them. Deborah, who is an artist, also designed the cover for this book, for which she deserves a special thanks. As Ben gets ready to vote in his first Presidential election – he just cast his first Congressional ballot in 2006 – I hope that he finds a process that is more welcoming and inclusive, with greater, not lesser, democratic control. For the happiness and joy they bring to me, I dedicate this book to them.

CHAPTER 1
Introduction

As the country headed into the 2004 presidential election, a survey of cable television viewers conducted by Peter Hart for C-SPAN found that Americans felt disconnected from government and ignored by the political process, with close to half saying they did not have any influence on what their government did.[1] And this was the opinion of a group—cable viewers make up 85 percent of the public—that is more interested in government and politics than might be expected if the other 15 percent of the public were added to the sample.[2]

And while the 2004 election itself did see an increase in voter turnout (reaching the highest levels since the 1960s), public disillusionment persisted. By October 2005, the approval rating for President George W. Bush hovered at 40 percent (with his more generic favorability rating at 46 percent), and the overall rating of the federal government was down to 45 percent, as was the favorability rating of Congress.[3] By April 2006, the figures were even worse: the president's job approval rating was down to 35 percent (and his favorability down to 40 percent); the percentage of those thinking Congress had done "less than usual" climbed to 41 percent (the highest number since 1997); only 47 percent of the public had a favorable view of the Democrats; and 40 percent held a favorable opinion of Republicans (both figures being the lowest recorded since 1992).[4]

Clearly, some of the distrust of and disconnect with government and politics reflects the perception of a particular government failure, in this case the war in Iraq, just as Vietnam, Watergate, and the Energy Crisis led to disillusionment in the past. But some of this—an important part, in fact—represents the continuation of a long, forty-year trend of declining connections between the public and the political system. This decline can be seen in many aspects of the relationship between citizens and government, but it is most easily observed in our participation in (or lack thereof) and feelings about our electoral process, the aspect of our system designed most directly to bring us, the public, into the political mainstream.

Democracy depends upon a healthy electoral process because it is such a process that allows citizens to be heard, that keeps government in check if it is doing things we do not approve of, and that pushes government to pursue the policies we would like to see enacted. And for at least forty years, we have slowly but surely seen our sense of democratic control of elections—in particular the presidential election, the most visible and involving of all of our elections—slip away. We participate less, we care less, and we feel less involved. Our sense that what we want matters to our elected officials declines, and we see fewer reasons to get involved. And this creates a vicious cycle, as more people drop out, giving those running for office and those already in office even less incentive to pay attention to what citizens want.

This book attempts to take a closer look at the systematic forces that have led to this loss of control. Its goal is to clarify why it is that we have seen our sense of democratic control slipping away beyond the particular failures of particular policies. For the danger to our democracy does not come from those failures. Government always has some success and some failure, but as long as our broader sense of the system is intact, we attempt to use our political influence to correct the failures and reward the successes. When our disillusionment grows too strong, our response to failure is no longer one of trying to change things, but one of resignation and apathy. Any changes that do occur reflect the interests of a narrower group of people with continuing influence and involvement, and the more narrow that group becomes, the less democracy we have.

What, then, are the root causes of this change? In the pages that follow, I will examine a number of forces that have slowly but surely eroded our sense of democratic control. Some of these forces revolve around changes in technology, as the growth and evolution of communications technology—in particular television and, later, computer technology—has changed the relationship among citizens, candidates, and government. Some of it, too, has to do with the rules and regulations we have that govern the way our electoral process works. In some cases we have changed the rules in ways that make the system less effective from a democratic perspective. (The most striking example here is the rules that govern the nomination part of election campaigns.) In other cases, rules that were created to make things more democratic were left with loopholes that were exploited over time and, in the end, seemed to make things worse (campaign finance being the primary example in this category). In still other cases, long time rules have interacted with other changes, in particular the changes in technology alluded to above, to make those rules more of a problem than they used to be. (The Electoral College, the body by which our president is chosen, is the prime example here.)

These changes have not occurred in a vacuum, nor have those concerned with democracy been absent from the scene. While our democracy has been in decline, that decline has not occurred because of a lack of effort to keep it vigorous and alive. In fact, over the past thirty years, those concerned with the state of democracy in our presidential election process have made a number of changes in the rules governing that process—both in the party rules concerning the nomination of candidates and in campaign finance regulations. And, for a time in the early 1970s, it seemed as if these rules might create a more open, egalitarian, public-driven process. Given the vast amount of information available to ordinary citizens, the rules mandating citizen participation in the selection of nominees by the major parties, and rules providing for public funding of much of the presidential election process, one would think we would have embarked on a golden era of citizen participation. But that did not happen. Instead, these changes have been overwhelmed by other trends in technology, growing public apathy (which is, in part, a function of the sense of a lack of control in the election process, but also a result of other factors), and the actions of other governmental bodies, in particular state legislatures and the courts. And this has produced a downward spiral in the public's influence in the selection of our nation's leader.

This book will focus on these trends, how they have seemingly spiraled out of control, and the continued risk they pose to our democracy. It will do so by examining what the current presidential election process is, how reformers hoped to help make that process more democratic and open, and why those reform efforts failed.

Chapter 2 will examine the rules of the nomination process. We will look at how reformers attempted, particularly in the aftermath of the 1968 Democratic National Convention in Chicago, to put in place a new set of rules designed to open up the process to public participation. The controversial and changing role of the Iowa Caucuses and the New Hampshire Primary is illustrative of the changes we will explore. There was a brief period in the mid-1970s when this process did seem to work as advertised. (The election of Jimmy Carter, a true outsider, was the high point in this regard, which is not to say that Carter was a successful president. Rather, the point is that his election reflected a system that seemed quite open to public influence.) But various other trends have resulted in a process where the key is now to raise lots of money early on, with an "invisible primary" that makes the nomination an almost foregone conclusion before the public even gets to weigh in with its views.

Chapter 3 will explore the issue of money in the presidential election process. The amendments to the Federal Election Campaign Finance Act of

1971 that were passed in the wake of the Watergate scandal in 1974 set up a system of public finance of the general presidential election and partial funding of the primaries. And again, for a while, this seemed to work. In 1976 and in the 1980s we had a series of elections where money was not a dominant force (at least not in presidential elections). But over time, increasing costs, the Supreme Court decision in *Buckley* v. *Valeo*, and changes in the law regarding "soft money" led to a situation where money had, once again, become dominant. This chapter will trace those changes and look at the impact of the newest attempt to reverse these trends, the Bipartisan Campaign Reform Act of 2002 (BCRA) that was passed in order to try, once again, to fix this area of political campaigns and which went into effect beginning with the 2004 election cycle. As we will see, some of the changes made by BCRA did, in fact, help. But others were counterproductive, and so while some trends in campaign finance improved from a democratic perspective, others did not.

Chapter 4 will look at the Electoral College. The rules governing this body have not changed since the passage of the Twelfth Amendment to the U.S. Constitution, but its impact has. We will examine the rules of this body and how they structure the way candidates run for the presidency. The Electoral College has always turned the election into a series of separate state elections. And candidates have always operated under the assumption that some states will be close, some states will be easily won, and some states will almost certainly be lost. But the development of technology—particularly polling and mass media—has made it increasingly easier to do more accurate targeting, and this has changed the nature of campaigns. In 1960, Richard Nixon promised to visit every state in the union as part of his campaign. No candidate today would dream of doing so. Instead, technology allows candidates to focus more and more effort on fewer, more strategic locations. Chapter 4 will also examine the changes that this has caused, looking at the travel schedules and media targeting of presidential candidates. The result of this is that much attention is lavished on a small number of voters, but larger and larger percentages of potential voters are ignored and made to feel as if they do not matter.

In chapter 5 we will take a closer look at how citizens have responded to these trends, examining the shifts in public attitude toward our presidential election and broader political processes over the past forty years. And we will examine how these changes have impacted the role of the organizations that act as intermediaries between citizens and the democratic process, interest groups, and political parties. The role of these organizations has changed dramatically over the past forty years. Interest groups have become more visible and active, and the political parties have shifted their behavior in important ways, many of which have led to further distancing of citizens from the electoral process.

But all is not lost. There are also reasons for hope. For forty years, most of these trends were uniformly negative, but as suggested already, the 2004 election provided a vision of how our electoral process might be reinvigorated, as some of these trends did seem to reverse themselves, at least temporarily. In chapter 6 we will examine the 2004 election in more detail, separating out those changes that seemed to be the result of the specific forces at work in that election from those that might represent more systematic changes in the relationship that we have with our democratic electoral process. And we will conclude with a look at the kinds of reforms that would help reconnect citizens with the electoral process by making the process more open to citizen control. Some of these reforms involve further changes in rules and procedures, but many of them involve tapping into the broader potential presented by the Internet, while others involve changing attitudes and practices in ways that maximize citizens' connection with the political world.

The road to stronger democratic control, to a system where the public feels as if it, not "special interests" are actually important in choosing our leaders, will not be swift or straight. But a clearer understanding of the barriers that confront us and the tools at our disposal can maximize our chances of reaching that destination as swiftly and as easily as possible. It is my hope that this book can help us along that road.

Notes

1. Reid, T.R., "Most Americans Feel They're on Sidelines of Political Process, Poll Finds," *The Washington Post*, 18 March 2004, A6, accessed on-line at http://www.washingtonpost.com/ac2/wp-dyn/A2853-2004Mar17?language=printer.
2. According to a study by the Pew Research Center for the People and the Press in April of 2004, for example, 45% of Cable Subscribers "read a newspaper yesterday," compared with only 31% of non-subscribers, while 62% had "watched TV news yesterday," compared to only 50% of non-subscribers." "On-Line News Audiences More Diverse," 8 June 2004. p. 49.
3. Pew Research Center for the People and the Press, "Public Sours on Government and

Business," 25 October 2005, available on-line at http://people-press.org/reports /display.php3?ReportID=261.

4 Pew Research Center for the People and the Press, "Public Disillusionment with Congress at Record Levels," 20 April 2006, available at http://people-press.org/reports /display.php 3?ReportID=275.

CHAPTER 2
The Nomination Process

The first stage (and in some ways the most important stage) of the presidential election process occurs when the two major parties choose their nominees. For all intents and purposes, this stage reduces the public's choice to two candidates. On rare occasions, a third-party candidate has done reasonably well in November. Then ex-President Theodore Roosevelt received 27 percent of the popular vote in 1912, the only time since the establishment of the Democratic and Republican Parties as the two major parties in the United States in 1860 that a third-party candidate outpolled one of the major parties. In 1992, Ross Perot received 19 percent of the popular vote. The only other third-party candidates to receive more than 10 percent of the vote since 1860 were Progressive Robert La Follette in 1924 (17 percent) and George Wallace in 1968 (14 percent). But in almost all cases, once the two parties have chosen their candidates, the voters have but two options. Thus, the process by which the Democrats and Republicans choose their nominees is paramount.

That process has been changed over time in an attempt to increase the role of the public in the selection of the party nominees. Up until 1968, the changes were gradual and incremental at best, but they saw a major shift in the 1970s. Since then, continuing efforts have been made to open up the system to allow the public a greater role, but all of these efforts have been overwhelmed by a combination of technology, unintended interactions between different kinds of efforts at different levels in the system, and with unintended consequences, to produce a system that causes much of the public to feel distressed and disenchanted. This nominating process, then, is the beginning of the public's alienation from the way we choose our chief executive.

A Brief History of the Nomination System, 1792–1932

There was no provision for party nominations in the initial election of George Washington. In fact, as we will see in chapter 4, some envisioned that the Electoral College would serve as a nominating mechanism, narrowing down the choices for the Congress to choose from. But the development of political parties quickly led to a need for those parties to have a mechanism for choosing their candidates for president. And the first body to play that role was the party caucus in Congress.[1] However, as more and more states changed their general election rules to allow the public to express its preference for a presidential candidate, the domination of the nomination process by congressional elites came under challenge. And in 1824 barely one-fourth of the Democratic-Republican members of Congress (as today's Democratic Party was then called) even showed up for their caucus meeting to nominate William Crawford for the presidency. A number of state legislatures put forward nominees as well, including John Quincy Adams by Massachusetts, Henry Clay by Kentucky, and Andrew Jackson by Tennessee. Jackson won the popular vote in the election, but no one won an Electoral College majority, and the House of Representatives chose Adams as president. Crawford finished fourth in the popular vote and third in the Electoral College, and the notion of congressional elites nominating candidates disappeared.

In 1828, the two major candidates, Andrew Jackson and President Adams, again relied on their state legislatures to nominate them for president. But in 1832, in an attempt to give more legitimacy to the selection process, the Democrats (as they were now called), following the lead of a minor party—the Anti-Masons—chose their nominee at a convention where representatives of the party from the various states came together to choose their candidate. This process, a convention of state party delegates meeting to choose a nominee, became the dominant feature of the system until the post-1968 reform era.

The Slow Rise of the National Party

While the convention of state and local party leaders was the dominant feature of the nominating system for 130 years, that time saw a slow evolution that reflected a growing nationalization of politics.[2] In the early years, conventions would depose incumbent presidents—John Tyler in 1844, Millard Filmore in 1852, and Franklin Pierce in 1856—and the locus of power resided within the state and local parties, who chose their delegates in any way that they desired. But a number of trends began to lead to calls for a more inclusive and regularized nominating system, including the nationalization of politics; the rise of a national media and the decline in power of local parties, at least in part as a result of the shift from a patronage to a civil service merit system, which began to cut off the lifeblood of local parties; and the perceived corruption of the party system.[3] As Alan Ware has made clear, the parties did not respond to these calls for change with outright hostility. Rather, they adapted to the calls for change and worked to tailor those changes in ways that would not challenge their ultimate authority over the political system. The parties tended to be supportive of, not implacably opposed to, reforms such as the adoption of the Australian ballot and the direct primary, though anti-party sentiment did shape the debate over these reforms.[4] As this nationalization occurred, the convention itself became less important, and the method of delegate selection took on a greater role.

The first state to mandate direct primaries to select delegates to the convention was Wisconsin in 1905,[5] and by 1912 there were twelve states using primaries to select delegates. But there was little growth after that, and by 1968 there were still only seventeen states using direct election to help choose the nominee.[6] Still, as the national media grew in importance and the nationalization of politics continued, would-be candidates learned that they could use a strong showing in the primaries to convince party leaders in other states that they were worthy of support. John Kennedy's use of his victories in Wisconsin and heavily Protestant West Virginia over rival Hubert Humphrey were instrumental in helping him secure the 1960 presidential nomination, lending legitimacy to the notion that delegates selected by the people were a particularly effective way for a candidate to show popular appeal.

Perhaps at least as important in establishing the legitimacy of primaries as a way to win convention delegates was the growth of television. Gavel-to-gavel coverage of the conventions had begun in the 1950s, and the parties soon discovered that the more harmony they displayed before the cameras, the better the party would look to the broader public. Thus, there was pressure to have the nomination all wrapped up prior to the convention. And no convention since the Republican National Convention in 1952 has gone to more than a single ballot. The convention had become a place to ratify the decisions made earlier, when delegates were chosen. This, too, made it more useful for potential candidates to show off their ability to win votes prior to the convention. Bargaining among party leaders at the convention was much less appealing. Still, the rules of the convention had to catch up to this reality.

In 1964, President Lyndon Johnson wanted a convention coronation. The Mississippi delegation to the convention was selected in a process that prohibited participation by African American citizens. Johnson was concerned about the way this would look, and when an alternative group calling itself the Mississippi Freedom Democratic Party announced that it would come to the convention in Atlantic City and demand to be seated instead of the official party delegation which, it said, was selected in a way that left African-American Democrats out of the process, the Johnson people imposed a compromise allowing two of the alternative delegates to be seated as part of the Mississippi delegation. This compromise did not satisfy either side, but it made clear that the national party would concern itself with the methods by which delegates were chosen, and that it wanted a process that was open to all potential party members. Furthermore, the convention passed a resolution forbidding discrimination in the selection of delegates, and when the Mississippi delegation arrived four years later without having followed this new requirement, the entire delegation was thrown out of the convention. The 1964 compromise and the relatively narrow rules banning racial discrimination in choosing delegates may not have seemed like much of a statement at the time, but four years later reformers—dissatisfied with a convention that nominated a candidate who did not win a single contested primary, Hubert Humphrey (all the contested primaries were won by either President Johnson, Eugene McCarthy, or Robert Kennedy)—demanded additional changes. And the Humphrey people, in an attempt to build party unity, agreed to set up a commission to examine the rules of the party that applied to the delegate selection process. The slow evolution of a system that was more and more concerned with allowing "ordinary citizens" to play a role in choosing the nominees was about to take a radical step forward. We need to take a closer look at that 1968 convention and the changes that it led to, for that chain of events set in motion the dynamic that has governed the nomination process ever since.

The 1968 Convention and the Reforms That Followed

The 1968 Democratic convention brought to a head many of the long-term trends that had been pushing the process in a direction that would involve more public participation as a way to legitimize the nomination selection proceedings.[7] Supporters of Robert Kennedy and Eugene McCarthy were distressed by the fact that Vice-President Humphrey had not won a single contested primary and used that to challenge the legitimacy of his nomination. The television coverage of the convention and the anti-war demonstrations in the streets of Chicago showed a party torn and, to many, under the control of people out of touch with the public. National party leaders felt a need to try to accommodate the dissidents and unify the party for the November election. And so, amid much confusion—according to Rhodes Cook, many of the delegates did not even realize what they were voting for[8]—the convention voted to set up a commission to review the party's nominating process.

This commission, usually referred to as the McGovern-Fraser Commission after the two commission chairs—first Senator George McGovern, who later resigned from the commission in order to run for the Democratic nomination, and then his replacement, Representative Donald Fraser—established a new set of rules for the party. The key to these rules was the desire to create a process that was seen as legitimate by the public by insuring the ability of the public to play a central role in that process. Essentially, the rules allowed for two different ways of choosing delegates: primary elections and open caucuses—that is, caucuses that were open to participation by anyone who thought of themselves as a member of the party, and not restricted to party leaders and their associates.[9]

The most important result of this rule was an increase in the number of states selecting delegates through primary election. That number jumped to twenty-three in 1972 and then to thirty in 1976. It has since grown to between thirty-five and forty, depending upon the year in question. The Democrats also prohibit winner-take-all primaries and require that any candidate gaining at least 15 percent of the vote receive a proportional number of delegates.[10] This, too, insures that more people feel as if they have a voice in the selection process. And the immediate result of this was a huge jump in the number of citizens involved in selecting convention delegates. The number of citizens participating in presidential primaries jumped from 12 million in 1968 to 22 million in 1972 to 26 million in 1976. That number has ranged from 25 million to 35 million since.[11] And even in those states holding caucuses, public participation has risen dramatically. The Iowa Caucuses, which attract approximately 100,000 to 125,000 voters per party if they are being contested, are the best example of this. Clearly, turnout in primaries is much higher than in caucuses, and turnout in caucuses after Iowa is much lower than in that state. Still, the system has opened up the process to many more people.

This process also solidified the change begun earlier when candidates, not party leaders, became the central actors in the nominating campaign. Where once the campaign was dominated by party officials, it was now dominated by candidates appealing directly to issue activists and other citizens.[12] John Kennedy had campaigned in primaries to convince party officials that he could win a general election. Now candidates campaigned in primaries to win the delegates to win the nomination directly. Their audience became the public, not the party. And this meant that those without strong ties to the party establishment had a much greater chance of winning the nomination. To those who had supported Robert Kennedy and, especially, Eugene McCarthy in 1968, this shift in power away from party officials, giving a greater role to the party's grass roots supporters and a greater likelihood of success to outsider or insurgent candidates, was precisely the kind of change that they wanted.

As a result, the increasing role of the media was reinforced. Coverage of the campaign became even more important. Winning, or doing well, created positive press that helped a candidate appeal to the public, increasing his or her chances of winning votes. This, in turn, exacerbated the problem of how the public might perceive a divided party. Media focus on such divisions were not good for the eventual nominee. This created an incentive to wrap up this very public battle for the nomination as soon as possible, an incentive that was evident to the candidates and party officials alike.[13] In addition, states found that waiting too long could eliminate their influence on the system. It made no sense to have a primary in April if the nomination was all but wrapped up in March; thus, states began to move their primary and caucus dates up closer to the beginning of the calendar, creating a process that has been labeled front-loading.[14]

When primaries were used prior to the 1968 reforms, the pattern tended to be one of a few primaries early and more toward the end of the process. Busch and Mayer document this change, noting that in 1960, for example, by five weeks into the primary season (that is, five weeks after the New Hampshire Primary), only two primaries had been held, representing 2 percent of the delegates to be chosen in primaries.[15] While the numbers do fluctuate, from 1952 to 1980 the percentage of delegates chosen in the first five weeks of the primary season only exceeded 20 percent one time—in 1952—when 22 percent of the Democratic delegates and 26 percent of the Republican delegates chosen by primaries had been selected by the fifth week of the season. But beginning in 1980, states began to move things up. On the Democratic side, the number jumped to 36 percent of the delegates and—after declining to 29 percent in 1984—climbed to 49 percent in 1988, 41 percent in 1992, and 60 percent in 1996. In 2000, in an attempt to stem the front-loading tide, the Democrats imposed a rule mandating a four-week waiting period after New Hampshire so that by the fifth week in 2000, only the 1 percent of the delegates chosen in primaries had been selected. But this rule change did little, as in the next two weeks an additional twenty states representing 64 percent of the delegates chosen by primaries had their contests. The Republican pattern is largely the same, though the drop-off in 2000 was not as great, since the mandated window of the Democrats did not apply, and six states representing 12 percent of the delegates did hold primaries in that time period. And like the Democrats, by week seven, two-thirds of the delegates had been selected.

It is also important to keep in mind that these front-loading figures may underestimate the effect in two ways. First, as the number of states using primaries has been increasing, the percentage of delegates chosen in primaries has also been increasing. For example, in the 1960s delegates chosen by primaries represented between 39 percent and 46 percent of the total number of delegates. In the 1970s that number jumped to between 61 percent and 74 percent of the delegates. And with the exception of 1984, that percentage has never dropped below 70 percent since then.[16] Second, the date of the New Hampshire Primary, the start of the primary season, has been moving forward as well. In 1960 the New Hampshire Primary was held on March 8. By 1996 it had moved forward to February 20. In 2000 it was held on February 1. And in 2004 it had been moved to January 27.

Thus, the post-1968 nomination system has become a candidate-centered, front-loaded process. The initial reforms led to a surge in the number of primaries and changed the nature of the remaining caucuses so that citizen-activists, not party officials, decided who would be the nominee, and the campaigns of the contenders for the nomination took center stage. As this process started, the primaries and caucuses were spread over a period of approximately four months. George McGovern in 1972, and both Jimmy Carter and Gerald Ford in 1976, needed important primary victories in some of the last states to choose delegates to win their nomination campaigns. But the dynamic of the process meant that states that held earlier primaries and caucuses were more likely to have a greater impact on the nomination, and that has led the system to evolve into a strongly front-loaded battle. As a result, the system has evolved in ways that have stymied the attempts of reformers to create a process wherein voters feel connected to the choices being made. We need to take a closer look at how this has occurred.

The Impact of the Reformed Nomination Process

Being Early Becomes Crucial. The nomination system places a heavy emphasis on the early contests, particularly the Iowa Caucuses and the New Hampshire Primary.[17] A candidate who wins these contests is not guaranteed victory, as John McCain, winner of the 2000 New Hampshire Primary, and George Bush, winner of the 1980 Iowa Caucuses, discovered. But doing badly in these contests, not meeting whatever expectations have been raised about a campaign's likely achievements, is almost always fatal. These two contests weed out the field, and candidates ignore them at great risk.[18] The importance of these two contests can be seen in a number of ways. First, they receive an inordinate amount of press coverage. A study of the 1980 nomination contest found that 28 percent of the coverage on the CBS Evening News and on the UPI wire was devoted to Iowa and New Hampshire, much more than any other states, especially when the small number of delegates at stake in those contests is taken into account.[19] Second, candidates and outside groups spend a disproportionate amount of money in these states. In 2000, for example, three of the candidates who accepted public matching funds and the expenditure limits that go with them—Al Gore, Bill Bradley, and Gary Bauer—spent up to the limit in Iowa, as did Gore, Bradley, and John McCain in New Hampshire, while the two candidates who did not accept public funds—George Bush and Steve Forbes—spent at least that much.[20] Similarly, in 2004, four of the candidates—John Kerry, John Edwards, Dick Gephardt, and Howard Dean—spent over $2 million in Iowa,[21] and four—Dean, Kerry, Wesley Clark, and Joseph Lieberman—spent over $600,000 for television ads in New Hampshire in just the final week of the campaign.[22] (We will take a closer look at the money issue in chapter 3.) Busch and Mayer found that in 1980, controlling for the unusual amount of spending in Iowa and New Hampshire, a state would add an additional $4,000 to $12,000 per day in total candidate spending for each day they moved their primary up toward the front of the election calendar.[23] Third, the candidates spend a disproportionate amount of time in these two states. According to figures compiled by Hugh Winebrenner and the Des Moines Register, for example, in 2004 five candidates spent more than fifty days in Iowa, led by Howard Dean with seventy-six visits.

Similarly, Steve Forbes spent eighty-three days in Iowa prior to the 2000 caucuses, while Lamar Alexander was in Iowa for seventy-nine days and Bill Bradley was there forty-eight times. And the record number of visits (not counting Iowa Senator Tom Harkin in 1992!) was Dick Gephardt in 1988, when he spent 148 days in Iowa.[24] This type of intensive campaigning in the small states of Iowa and New Hampshire means that a surprisingly large proportion of citizens actually meets at least one of the presidential candidates. In 2000, for example, three weeks before the caucuses, 39 percent of registered Democrats and 34 percent of registered Republicans had met at least one of the candidates.[25] Similarly, in 1996, 20 percent of likely New

Hampshire Republican Party primary voters had met a candidate, and nearly 70 percent had either met a candidate or received a call or mailing from a candidate.[26]

TABLE 2-1: Candidate Visits to Iowa	
Howard Dean	76
John Kerry	73
Dick Gephardt	67
John Edwards	64
Dennis Kucinich	54
Bob Graham	22
Joseph Lieberman	16
Carol Moseley Braun	13
Al Sharpton	7
Wesley Clark	3
Figure is the number of days from January 1, 2003, up through caucus night, January 19, 2004, on which the candidate made an appearance in the state as counted by the *Des Moines Register*. Accessed at DesMoinesRegister.com/extras/politics/caucus2004/days.html.	

Thus, in Iowa and New Hampshire, one finds an intensive, democratic experience that allows citizens both the time and information to make informed decisions about who should be their party's nominee. While money does matter, a topic we will return to in chapter 3, retail door-to-door direct contact campaigning (in person, by phone, and through mailings and literature drops) is much more important than it is in larger states with more compressed campaign schedules. Candidates in Iowa and New Hampshire regularly show up for meetings of seventy-five or one hundred (or sometimes twenty-five!) people. A candidate with no media presence is still at a major disadvantage, but a media presence without retail campaigning is also likely to fail.

This allows, in theory, a less-well-known candidate to campaign on a relatively small budget: even with the increased spending of recent years, Iowa and New Hampshire are relatively inexpensive states in which to campaign, especially when compared to more populous states such as California, New York, or Texas. And in the early years of the reformed process, George McGovern in 1972 and Jimmy Carter in 1976 used this strategy to win the nomination. They spent a lot of time in Iowa and New Hampshire, did well in those states, and used that success to raise the money needed to run campaigns in later primaries and caucuses, allowing them to defeat much more established—and resource-rich—candidates. But front-loading seems to be diminishing this possibility with each election cycle, as unknown outsider candidates no longer have the time to use a surprise showing in Iowa and/or New Hampshire to build up the resources they need to challenge more favored, insider candidates.

Still, citizens in Iowa and New Hampshire are in a position to learn about the candidates.[27] And, as Larry Bartels has shown, as voters learn more about the candidates, they base their decisions on more substantive matters.[28] In these states, we have the material needed for voters to become effective democratic citizens.

And voters do respond. Turnout in these two states is remarkably high. Clearly, caucuses will have significantly lower turnout than primaries, and Iowa, even with these advantages, is no exception.[29] Turnout in Iowa lags far behind turnout in primary states. A "good turnout" for the caucuses will be between 100,000 and 125,000 per party. And in 2000, turnout was approximately 11 percent of the turnout in Iowa in the general election.[30] But in New Hampshire, turnout is higher than any other state. By Cook's measurement, New Hampshire turnout in 2000 was 69 percent of the New Hampshire general election turnout. Only California, at 68 percent, was above 60 percent, and only three other states were above 50 percent.[31] Using the more traditional measure of turnout as a percentage of the voting-age population, Mayer reports New Hampshire Republican turnout in 2000 at 42 percent. Turnout in the states over the next month averaged 26 percent, as did turnout on "Super Tuesday," a Tuesday when a number mostly Southern states coordinated their early primaries and caucuses in order to maximize their impact, while turnout after that date averaged 16 percent. On the Democratic side, he found New Hampshire turnout to be 40 percent, Super Tuesday turnout to average 17 percent (the Democrats did not allow primaries between New Hampshire and Super Tuesday), and turnout after that to be 16 percent.[32] So we end up with a trade-off. We have two small states where voters are treated to all of the advantages of inclusive, deliberative democracy. But as front-loading has made it more and more difficult for candidates to stay in the race long enough to reach out to voters in other places, the overall system seems less and less connected to ordinary voters.

The Long Campaign That Nobody Sees. As the turnout figures cited above indicate, voter interest in the nomination campaign tends to fall off rapidly. By the time many states vote, the nomination is already locked up. After a sharp overall rise in participation from 11 percent of the voting-age population voting in primaries in 1968, to a peak of 21 percent in 1988, the number declined to 15 percent in 2000.[33] (All three of those elections—1968, 1988, and 2000—had no incumbent, maximizing the likelihood of contested primaries and higher turnout.) In fact, in 2000, twenty-five states had their primaries after John McCain and Bill Bradley had withdrawn from the race, leaving only one candidate, the eventual nomination winner, as the option.

Candidates know that they must start the campaign much earlier. As Steven Wayne notes, it is now almost standard practice to begin testing the presidential waters two years before the actual election.[34] Howard Dean was the first candidate to form an official advisory committee to begin the campaign process for 2004, beginning in the early fall of 2002. He was quickly followed by John Kerry. And once Vice-President Gore announced that he would not seek the nomination in December 2002, a number of other candidates, including Dick Gephardt, John Edwards, Tom Daschle, Joseph Lieberman, and Bob Graham, also set up campaign committees. And it just keeps getting earlier. In the summer of 2006, before the 2006 mid-term elections, at least nine potential candidates visited Iowa in the month of August, with most stopping by the Iowa State Fair.[35]

Similarly, early fundraising has become even more important. By December 31, 2003, before the beginning of the year in which the actual election began, the various candidates for president had raised $268 million (compared with $151 million by December 31, 1999). Almost half of that was raised by President Bush ($132 million), with the rest divided among ten Democratic candidates, one of whom, Bob Graham, had already dropped out of the race.[36]

The tight schedule that begins with the Iowa caucuses puts enormous pressure on the candidates to jump out early. Thus, the "hidden campaign" becomes much less hidden. Candidates raise money and "go public" with their campaigns early. And much of their organizing now takes place not behind the scenes, but out in the open over the Internet. As Michael Cornfield and Jonah Seiger have written, "the Internet has made enough of the candidates' actions and insiders' conversations about those actions public as to render this process [the invisible campaign] of angling for advantage *visible*."[37] Howard Dean's campaign was the most innovative and successful at this stage, using the web to raise unprecedented and unexpected amounts of money and using cyberspace to create a traditional face-to-face political organization by drawing supporters together in "meet-up" events. Seeing Dean's success, as he not only pulled ahead in money, but also went from an unknown former governor of a small New England state to the front-runner in national polls, caused the other candidates to play catch-up. And by the time the primaries and caucuses got under way, just about all of them were engaged in a campaign where the Internet was at the center of their organizing activities.

TABLE 2-2: Early Fundraising in the 2004 Campaign

Candidate	Money Raised as of 12/31/03
George W. Bush	$132,124,843
Howard Dean	$41,043,489
John Kerry	$22,006,595
Richard Gephardt	$16,607,735
John Edwards	$16,423,300
Joseph Lieberman	$13,946,463
Wesley Clark	$13,804,560
Dennis Kucinich	$6,300,931
Bob Graham	$4,942,589
Carol Moseley Braun	$492,284
Al Sharpton	$396,365

The fundraising data comes from the Federal Election Commission. Reports from the campaigns can be found on-line at the FEC website (www.fec.org).

The subsequent failure of the Dean campaign and its rapid demise might seem to indicate that the importance of this part of the process was overestimated, but that is far from the truth. Rather, Dean's emergence as the front-runner showed how an unknown candidate can use a very visible "invisible primary" season to go from unknown to front-runner. It also created a situation in which other candidates had little hope but to use the early contests to catapult to the front and begin to raise the much larger sums of money that were needed in succeeding primary states. And Dean's quick demise, from front-runner to also-ran in one week, showed how the front-loaded system leaves little time for candidates to present themselves to the broader public outside the two early states of Iowa and New Hampshire.

Similarly, the experiences of Joseph Lieberman, Richard Gephardt, and, to a lesser extent, Wesley Clark, showed the unforgiving nature of the front-loaded process. Gephardt fell victim to his expectations in Iowa, where he was the early favorite. His fourth-place finish there ended his campaign. Similarly, Lieberman and Clark bypassed Iowa, spending enormous amounts of time in New Hampshire, with Lieberman actually renting an apartment in Manchester, living in the state for over a month. Their poor showings there left them basically out of the race, though Lieberman hung on for one more week before dropping out, and Clark was able to turn a very small victory (by barely 1,000 votes) in Oklahoma, another state where he spent much more time than any other candidate, into another week of campaigning before he finally left the race.

Once again, by the time most voters were choosing, the race had been determined. And in spite of the coverage in the national press, many voters were just beginning to make up their minds when the choices were made for them in Iowa, New Hampshire, and, to a lesser extent, the other early primaries. According to a CNN/USA/Gallup poll in the first week of 2004, large percentages of national voters either had never heard of or had no opinion of most of the leading Democratic candidates.[38]

Because of his place on the ticket in 2000, Joseph Lieberman was the best-known candidate, but even then, one-fourth of the public either did not know who he was or had no positive or negative feelings about him, and the least-known of these candidates, John Edwards, elicited the same response from over half the public. The voters of Iowa and New Hampshire may have had a good look at the candidates, but the rest of the nation did not. According to the *Des Moines Register*, Howard Dean, as noted above, spent seventy-six days in Iowa in the year leading up to the Iowa Caucuses, while John Kerry was in Iowa on seventy-three days, Dick Gephardt sixty-seven days, and John Edwards sixty-four days. (See table 2-1.) Lieberman and Clark, as noted above, bypassed Iowa and focused their attention on New Hampshire. But that means that the shape of the race became very clear before most voters had the chance to look closely at the candidates, and by the time they did get a look, the nomination battle was essentially over.

In 2004, then, John Kerry, and to a lesser extent John Edwards, were able to use their "surprisingly strong" showings in Iowa to catapult them to success in New Hampshire (Kerry), South Carolina (Edwards), and other early states (Missouri, Delaware, Arizona, New Mexico, and North Dakota, all of which went to Kerry) to become the major candidates for the nomination. In Kerry's case, he went from being almost written off in late December to the front-runner and prohibitive favorite within two weeks of the Iowa Caucuses. And Edwards went from a candidate with some potential but seemingly "too inexperienced" to be much of a factor, to the most serious challenger Kerry faced. In the final Gallup tracking poll in New Hampshire before the Iowa Caucuses (January 17–19), Kerry trailed Dean 32 percent to 25 percent, with Clark at 21 percent and Edwards at 7 percent.[39] Eight days later, the results found Kerry up to 38 percent, Dean at 26 percent, Clark and Edwards both at 12 percent. And one week later, Edwards was able to win a comfortable victory in South Carolina—45 percent to Kerry's 30 percent—to solidify his position as the major challenger to Kerry, a challenge that was ultimately unsuccessful.

TABLE 2-3: Pct. of People Without Views on the Candidates, Jan. 2004

		Never Heard Of:	No Opinion:
John Kerry	National Adults	19%	18%
	Democrats	20%	17%
John Edwards	National Adults	27%	25%
	Democrats	28%	21%
Joseph Lieberman	National Adults	10%	15%
	Democrats	11%	15%
Dick Gephardt	National Adults	18%	15%
	Democrats	21%	15%
Howard Dean	National Adults	17%	16%
	Democrats	17%	16%
Wesley Clark	National Adults	21%	16%
	Democrats	22%	18%

Democrats include Democratic leaners.
The figures come from the Gallup poll conducted January 2–5, 2004. The results were found at www.gallup.com/poll/releases/pr040107.asp.

Candidates can still use the retail politics of Iowa and New Hampshire to help bring them national attention and become viable candidates, but the front-loaded nature of the process leaves little room for error. If they do not have the money on hand to exploit such an opportunity, the window of opportunity will quickly close. Thus, the pre-primary money race becomes at least as important as the retail politics of Iowa and New Hampshire.

Conclusion

In the end, then, the nominating process has evolved into a system that leaves many citizens disenfranchised and dissatisfied. In spite of efforts to open the system up to the participation of the broader public, the evolution of a front-loaded process has created a nomination sequence that is both too long and too short. The candidates need to start raising money and campaigning early, almost as soon as the mid-term election is over, if not sooner. But since the money chase occurs among hardcore supporters and traditional party financiers, and the early campaigning is largely confined to Iowa and New Hampshire, most citizens are only beginning to pay attention to the contest when the final decision is made. Thus, citizens find the process too long (articles and television stories about the campaign begin two years prior to the election), but also find that they have little or no role to play in that process unless they happen to live in Iowa or New Hampshire.

Changing this part of the system to allow greater citizen participation, however, is not an easy thing to do. Proposals for reform that would lead to more citizens having a vote that counts in the system—a single nationwide primary is the most common reform in this direction, as it would potentially allow all citizens to play an equal role—run up against the problem that such changes would almost inevitably increase the importance of money, and the role of money is another aspect of the system that the public finds problematic. With such a reform, the gains of increasing the role of the public would be outweighed by the greater role that money would play, as such a change would dramatically widen the audience a candidate needs to reach quickly, forcing a reliance on expensive campaign advertisements. Starting in Iowa and New Hampshire allows candidates with relatively small amounts of money to do well and use the momentum from those states to raise enough cash to compete on a wider stage. This aspect of the system is something those concerned with effective democracy would want to keep.[40] And there may, in fact, be reforms that could strike a better balance, potentially improving the amount and quality of involvement by the public in the process without unduly increasing the importance of money and those who contribute money to the campaign. We will examine some of these potential reforms in chapter 6, but before we do so, we need to take a closer look at the role of money in both the nomination contest and the general election that follows.

Notes

1 Many books on the history of political parties in the United States outline the changes in the nominating process. A good example is found in chapter 2 of White, John Kenneth, and Shea, Daniel, *New Party Politics: From Jefferson and Hamilton to the Information Age*, 2nd ed. (Belmont, CA: Thompson/Wadsworth, 2004). Also, see ch. 1 of Wayne, Steven, *The Road to the White House 2004* (New York: Bedford/St. Martin's, 2004); and ch. 2 of Cook, Rhodes, *The Presidential Nominating Process, A Place for Us?* (Lanham, MD: Rowman & Littlefield, 2004).

2 The best discussion of the history of presidential nominations is Shafer, Byron, *Bifurcated Politics* (Cambridge, MA: Harvard University Press, 1988).

3 See Shafer, *Bifurcated Politics*, esp. ch. two.

4 See Ware, Alan, *The American Direct Primary* (New York: Cambridge University Press, 2002), especially part three. For a more traditional view of how anti-party sentiment contributed to the push for changes in the nominating process, see Ranney, Austin, *Curing the Mischiefs of Faction: Party Reform in America* (Berkeley: University of California Press, 1975).

5 Florida, in 1901, had passed legislation allowing the Democratic Party to choose delegates by direct election if the party wanted to do so, but Wisconsin was the first to mandate such a system.

6 There were only fifteen Republican primaries in 1968. In the discussion here I will concentrate on the Democratic Party, since it was their reforms that drove the process I am describing. As we will see later, changes on the Republican side would also make a difference, but in the early reform years, the Democratic Party took the lead.

7 There are many strong accounts of the 1968 convention and the reforms it engendered. Among the best are Shafer, Byron, *Quiet Revolution: The Struggle for the Democratic Party and the Shaping of Post-Reform Politics* (New York: Russell Sage Foundation, 1983), and Polsby, Nelson, *Consequences of Party Reform* (New York: Oxford University Press, 1983). Among the many books with more extended looks at the presidential election process and the role of political parties in that process that put these changes and their impact into a broader context, aside from those in notes 1 and 4 above, are Abramowitz, Alan, *Voice of the People: Elections and Voting in the United States* (Boston: McGraw-Hill, 2004); Polsby, Nelson, and Wildavsky, Aaron, *Presidential Elections*, 10th ed. (New York: Chatham House, 2000); and White and Shea, *New Party Politics: From Jefferson and Hamilton to the Information Age*.

8 Cook, *The Presidential Nominating Process*, 43.

9 The actual rules were, and are, quite complicated. There were, for example, many rules about how primaries and caucuses could be structured. And those rules have changed in their particulars many times since 1972. My purpose here is not to go into the details of the rules and each particular change that occurred, or what these rules do and do not allow. Rather, in the discussion that follows, I want to highlight the central features of the procedure put in place by these rules and how that relates to this issue of public involvement and legitimacy. For more detailed discussion of the rules see the works referred to in note 7 above.

10 The lower threshold of 15 percent was, at one time, set at a higher 20 percent level. It was reduced to 15 percent after 1984 as a concession to Jesse Jackson supporters, who found that the 20 percent level resulted in their being underrepresented at the convention, since there were quite a few states where Jackson's vote totals fell between 15 and 20 percent. The Republicans do allow winner-take-all primaries, though since much of this is controlled by state law, most states, when adopting these provisions, ended up with laws that had both parties following the Democrats' rules.

11 See table 3.1 in Cook, *The Presidential Nominating Process*, adapted from *Congressional Quarterly's Guide to U.S. Elections*, 49. The ups and downs in turnout, aside from the impact of changes in the process that will be discussed below, are partly a function of how many candidates were running and which of the two parties had contested primaries. Thus, 1988, with no incumbent running, has the highest vote totals.

12 See Shafer, *Bifurcated Politics*, ch. 3. Also see Kirkpatrick, Jeane, *The New Presidential Elite* (New York: Russell Sage, 1976); Abramowitz, Alan, and Stone, Walter, *Nomination Politics: Party Activists and Presidential Choice* (New York: Praeger, 1984); Shafer, Byron, "Partisan Elites: 1946–1996," ch. 3 of Shafer, Byron, ed., *Partisan Approaches to Postwar American Politics* (New York: Chatham House, 1998); and Bernstein, Jonathan, "The *New* New Presidential Elite," in Mayer, William, ed., *In Pursuit of the White House 2000* (New York: Chatham House, 2000).

13 This reflects the so-called "divisive primary" hypothesis that such primaries hurt the party in the general election. The earliest discussion of this theory is Hacker, Andrew, "Does a 'Divisive' Primary Harm a Candidate's Election Chances?," *American Political Science Review* 59 (1965): 105–110. Arguments supporting this theory include Bernstein, Robert, "Divisive Primaries Do Hurt: U.S. Senate Races, 1956–1972," *American Political Science Review* 71 (1977): 540–45; Kenney, Patrick, and Rice, Tom, "The Effect of Primary Divisiveness in Gubernatorial and Senatorial Elections," *Journal of Politics* 46 (1984): 904–15; and Lengle, James; Owen, Diana; and Sonner, Molly, "Divisive Nominating Mechanisms and Democratic Party Electoral Prospects," *Journal of Politics* 57 (1995): 370–83. Others, however, have challenged the accuracy of this theory. For the argument that the impact of divisive primaries is not strong, see, among others, Johnson, Donald, and Gibson, James, "The Divisive Primary Revisited: Primary Activists in Iowa," *American Political Science Review* 68 (1984): 67–77; Stone, Walter, "The Carryover Effect in Presidential Elections," *American Political Science Review* 80 (1986): 271–80; and Atkeson, Lonna, "Divisive Primaries and General Election Outcomes: Another Look at Presidential Campaigns," *American Journal of Political Science* 42 (1998): 256–71. For a good summary of the entire debate that comes to the conclusion that divisive primaries are unlikely to be a key factor in determining general election outcomes except under some very particular (and highly unlikely) circumstances, see Atkeson, Lonna, "From the Primaries to the General Election: Does a Divisive Nomination Race Affect a Candidate's Fortunes in the Fall?," in Mayer, *In Pursuit of the White House 2000*, 285–312. But even if what Atkeson calls the "revisionist argument" against the importance of divisive primaries is correct, the widespread belief that it was correct is what governed the behavior of those seeking to move up the decision point of the process. The belief that a delayed decision would hurt the party might be mistaken, but if so,

that mistaken belief was still the basis for many to want to figure out how to wrap up the nomination battle in a timely manner.

14 The best discussion of the development and impact of front-loading is Mayer, William, and Busch, Andrew, *The Front-Loading Problem in Presidential Nominations* (Washington, DC: Brookings Institution, 2004). Also see Busch, Andrew, and Mayer, William, "The Front-Loading Problem," in Mayer, William, ed., *The Making of the Presidential Candidates 2004* (Lanham, MD: Rowman & Littlefield, 2004), 1–44, or the more general discussions in Wayne, *The Road to the White House 2004*; and Cook, *The Presidential Nominating Process*.

15 These figures and those that follow come from tables 1.1, 1.3, and 1.4 in Busch and Mayer, "The Front-Loading Problem," in Mayer, *The Making of the Presidential Candidates 2004*, 3, 5, and 6.

16 These figures can be found in table 7.1 in Wayne, Steven, *Is This Any Way to Run A Democratic Election* (Boston: Houghton Mifflin, 2001), 140.

17 The best study of the Iowa Caucuses is Winebrenner, Hugh, *The Iowa Precinct Caucuses: The Making of a Media Event*, 2nd ed. (Ames: Iowa State University Press, 1998). For the New Hampshire Primary, see Palmer, Niall, *The New Hampshire Primary and the American Electoral Process* (Westport, CT: Praeger, 1997); Brereton, Charles, *First in the Nation: New Hampshire and the Premier Presidential Primary* (Portsmouth, NH: Peter Randall, 1987); and Buell, Emmett, Jr., "The Changing Face of the New Hampshire Primary," in Mayer, *In Pursuit of the White House 2000*, 87–144.

18 Candidates will occasionally skip one of these contests. It is rarely a good idea. John McCain's strategy to skip Iowa and concentrate on New Hampshire in 2000 is the most successful attempt to bypass one of these contests. Others who have tried, such as Al Gore in 1988, have been much less successful. The only time one of these contests had little or no impact was in 1992 in Iowa, when Iowa Senator Tom Harkin's campaign overwhelmingly won the Iowa Caucuses. But because of his favorite-son status, every other candidate in the race stayed away—as, to a large extent, did the press—and those who stayed away suffered no ill effects. More important, Harkin got no benefit from his victory.

19 Robinson, Michael, and Sheehan, Margaret, *Over the Wire and on TV: CBS and UPI in Campaign '80* (New York: Russell Sage Foundation, 1983), 176–77.

20 See Redlawsk, David, and Sanders, Arthur, "Groups and the Grassroots in the Iowa Caucuses"; and Fowler, Linda; Spiliotes, Constantine; and Vavreck, Lynn, "Group Advocacy in the 2000 New Hampshire Primary," both in *PS: Political Science and Politics* 34, no. 2, June 2001, 270, 272 for the abstracts. The full texts are at www.apsanet.org/PS/June01/redlawsk.cfm and www.apsanet.org/PS/June01/fowler.cfm.

21 See Sanders, Arthur, "The Impact of BCRA on the Presidential Nomination Process: The 2004 Iowa Caucuses," in Magleby, David; Monson, Quin; and Patterson, Kelly, eds., *Dancing Without Partners* (Lanham, MD: Rowman & Littlefield, 2006), ch. 3.

22 Anderson, Nick, "Democrats Spend $3.5 Million on N.H. Primary Ad Blitz," *The Los Angeles Times*, 27 January 2004, accessed at http://www.latimes.com/news/nation/la-na-ads27jan27,1,5037374.story?coll=la-headlines-nation. And John Edwards spent over $400,000.

23 Busch and Mayer, "The Front-Loading Problem," 11.

24 Winebrenner, *The Iowa Precinct Caucuses*, and the *Des Moines Register*'s "Caucus Watch 2004," webpage at DesMoinesRegister.com/extras/politics/caucus2004/days.html.

25 Zelany, Jeff, "A Third in Iowa Poll Meet, Hear Candidates," *Des Moines Register*, 10 January 2000, A1.

26 Buhr, Tami, "What Voters Know about the Candidates and How They Learn It: The 1996 New Hampshire Republican Primary as a Case Study," in Mayer, *In Pursuit of the White House 2000*, 203–54. For an expansive look at the contact between grass-roots citizens and the candidates in the New Hampshire Primary, see Duncan, Dayton, *Grass Roots: One Year in the Life of the New Hampshire Presidential Primary* (New York: Viking Penguin, 1991).

27 For the best study of this, see Buhr, "What Voters Know About the Candidates and How They Learn It."

28 Bartels, Larry, *Presidential Primaries and the Dynamics of Public Choice* (Princeton, NJ: Princeton University Press, 1988).

29 See Redlawsk and Sanders, "Groups and the Grassroots in the Iowa Caucuses."

30 Cook, *The Presidential Nominating Process*, 96.

31 Ibid.

32 Busch and Mayer, "The Front-Loading Problem," 33.

33 Wayne, *The Road to the White House 2004*, 114.

34 Ibid., 119.

35 The nine included five Democrats: Gov. Tom Vilsack of Iowa, John Edwards, Evan Bayh, Joseph Biden, and John Kerry. The four Republicans were John McCain, Mitt Romney, George Pataki, and Newt Gingrich. See Beaumont, Thomas, "9 Potential Presidential Candidates Plan Trips," *Des Moines Register*, 1 August 2006, accessed at http://desmoines register.com/apps/pbcs.dll/article?AID=/20060801/NEWS09/60801038 1/1056.

36 The fundraising data comes from the Federal Election Commission. Reports from the campaigns can be found on-line at the FEC website (www.fec.org).

37 Cornfield, Michael, and Seiger, Jonah, "The Net and the Nomination," in Mayer, *The Making of the Presidential Candidates 2004*, 212. Italics in original.

38 The figures come from the Gallup poll conducted 2–5 January 2004. The results were found at www.gallup.com/poll/releases/pr040107.asp.

39 These figures are found at www.gallup.com/poll/releases/pr040126.asp.

40 Clearly, in this regard, it would not have to be Iowa and New Hampshire. Any small state where retail politics could make a difference would do.

CHAPTER 3
The Corrupting Influence of Money

Nothing makes the public feel less connected to the political system than the feeling that it is the money of large contributors and special interests, not the voters that matters to political leaders. And the sense that special interests hold too much power has been present for quite some time. For example, the American National Election series of public opinion surveys in election years found that the percentage of people agreeing that public officials do not care what people think was over 50 percent from 1986 through 2000, with a low of 51 percent in 1988 and a high of 66 percent in 1994. The post-September 11 rally of support for government saw a large drop in this figure in 2002 to 31 percent, but that number had risen back to 50 percent by 2004.[1] Similarly, the percentage of people who think the government is run for a few big interests, as seen in table 3.1, has, with the exception of the post-September 11 survey in 2002, been above 50 percent since 1970.

This concern for the role of special interests and their use of money to get their way has led to many efforts to control campaign finance. But while these efforts have had some temporary successes, the laws have not been able to stem the tide of the increasing role played by money, and those who can provide it, in the electoral process. Before looking at the most recent attempt to stem the influence of money, the Bipartisan Campaign Finance Reform Act of 2002 (BCRA), we need to look at the history and development of campaign finance legislation in order to place current efforts into the proper context.

The Rules of Campaign Finance

Concern about the role of money and its corrupting influence has been present since the early days of the Republic.[2] Political parties and candidates would often literally pay people to cast ballots for them, a practice made much more difficult by the adoption of the state-produced secret Australian ballot around the turn of the twentieth century.[3] And the practice of asking corporations for direct contributions to campaigns was ended with the passage of the Corrupt Practices Act in 1907, which made contributions from corporate treasuries illegal, a prohibition that was extended to unions with the passage of the Taft-Hartley Act in 1940. But most attempts at campaign finance reform were more loophole than law. For example, in an attempt to discourage large contributions, gifts over a particular amount to a campaign were treated as taxable income for the campaign committee. But all this did was lead to candidates setting up multiple committees so that a rich donor could write separate, tax-free gifts to "Nixon for President," "West Virginians for Nixon for President," "Lawyers for Nixon for President," etc.

TABLE 3-1: Is Government Run by a Few Big Interests?: 1964–2004

1964	29%	1984	55%
1966	33%	1988	64%
1968	40%	1990	71%
1970	50%	1992	75%
1972	53%	1994	76%
1974	66%	1996	69%
1976	66%	1998	64%
1978	67%	2000	61%
1980	70%	2002	48%
1982	61%	2004	56%

Source: American National Election Studies.
The data can be found at: www.umich.edu/~nes/nesguide/toptable/tab5a_2.htm.
The question asked was: "Would you say the government is pretty much run by a few big interests looking out for themselves or that it is run for the benefit of all people?" The question was not asked in 1986.
The percentage listed in the table is those agreeing that the government is run for a few big interests.

The beginning of the television era and improvements in other communications and travel technology through the 1960s led to rapidly rising costs for political campaigns. In the 1952 and 1956 elections, Adlai Stevenson and Dwight Eisenhower spent a combined total of $12 million (1952) and $13 million (1956). In 1960, Richard Nixon and John Kennedy spent $20 million; in 1964 Lyndon Johnson and Barry Goldwater spent $25 million; and in 1968 the combined total of Richard Nixon and Hubert Humphrey jumped to $37 million.[4] And this led Congress to pass the Federal Election Campaign Act of 1971 (FECA). However, in order to prevent Richard Nixon from killing the bill with a presidential veto, most provisions of the bill were not scheduled to take effect until the 1976 election. But before the law went into effect, Watergate happened, which prompted a major overhaul of the law.[5] The amendments to FECA in 1974 ushered in the contemporary campaign finance regime. The law had four major sections: disclosure, contribution limits, expenditure limits, and a system of voluntary public funding for presidential elections. The law was immediately challenged in court, and in 1976, in the landmark case of *Buckley* v. *Valeo* (424 U.S. 1), the Court upheld some of the law but overturned other portions, leaving in place a patchwork that eventually began to collapse.[6]

The disclosure provisions, which the Court upheld, required each candidate for federal office to designate a single finance committee that was required to disclose all of its income and expenditures. The goal here was transparency. The public should know where candidates get their funding. And over the years, technology has improved the effectiveness of this section of the law. The stacks of paper that would be filed in the 1970s, taking weeks to process and make public, have been replaced by mandatory on-line filing, creating searchable databases that are almost instantly available at the Federal Election Commission (FEC) website for those who want to look. And while ordinary citizens may not often take advantage of this capability, the press and watchdog groups such as the Campaign Finance Institute or the Center for Responsive Politics can and do. Who is spending how much and where the money is coming from is easy to discover.[7]

The second section of the law, also upheld by the Court, dealt with contribution limits. The amount that any individual could give to a candidate for federal office was limited to $1,000 per election.[8] The goal here was to prevent undue influence by large contributors. In addition to the limits on what individuals could give to campaigns, there were limits on the amount that individuals could contribute to political action committees (PACs), groups set up to influence political campaigns,[9] and to political parties. And there were limits on what PACs and parties could give to campaigns.

Third, there were expenditure ceilings designed to limit the cost of campaigning and prevent one candidate from vastly outspending her or his opponent. And there were limits on how much money groups could spend independently of a campaign or party to influence a campaign, limits on how much a party could spend in coordination with a campaign, and limits on how much of his or her own money a candidate could spend. But the Court struck down these expenditure limits as a violation of the First Amendment right of candidates and groups to express themselves. This ruling, as we will see in a moment, put pressure on the system and led to its eventual collapse.

In addition, the law was amended in 1979 to allow parties to raise and spend money outside of the provisions of the law, as long as it was used for specific non-election "party-building" activities such as voter registration and get-out-the-vote drives. This money was called "soft money" to distinguish it from "hard money," party funds raised according to FECA regulations that could be targeted toward specific elections.

Finally, there was a system of voluntary public funding for presidential elections that the Court also allowed to stand. Under this system, candidates for president would agree to take public funds. In the general election, there was to be full funding of major-party candidates, defined as those parties receiving more than 25 percent of the vote in the previous election (though parties could also qualify retroactively for the current election). The amount was set at $20 million in 1974 and indexed to inflation. By 2004 it had reached close to $75 million.[10] Candidates were allowed to raise additional funds, subject to contribution limits, to pay for legal, accounting, and compliance costs, but the cost of the campaign was supposed to be covered entirely from these public funds. No additional funds were to be raised or spent. Minor parties qualified for a prorated amount based on their showing in the previous election. They were permitted to raise and spend additional funds up to the overall limit. In the primaries, candidates could qualify for matching funds. In order to qualify, a candidate needed to raise at least $5,000 in contributions of $250 or less in at least twenty different states. Once qualified, the federal government matches the first $250 contributed by an individual donor. Candidates can still accept contributions from PACs and party committees, but these funds are not matched. And candidates accepting this public money must agree not to spend more than $50,000 of their own money. The idea behind this structure is to encourage a broad base of relatively small donors. As with the general election, taking public funds subjects the candidates to spending limits. The base ceiling was set in 1974 at $10 million and indexed to inflation. That figure had grown to $37 million in 2004. In addition, candidates can raise and spend a proportion of those funds to cover the costs of fundraising (20 percent of the base) and compliance (15 percent of the base). The total amount allowed in 2004,[11] then, was approximately $50 million. Finally, in addition to these overall limits, there are limits on how much can be spent in each state. The state-by-state limits are based on a formula established in 1974 that allows 16 cents times a state's voting-age population, with adjustments for inflation. These state limits in 2004 ranged from a low of $746,000 in Wyoming to a high in California of

$15 million. These limits are not related to the timing of the political calendar that makes spending in small, early states such as New Hampshire and Iowa more important than spending in larger states that come later in the process. In 1991 the FEC liberalized its rules for allocating expenses to state limits, making these limits more of an accounting issue than a meaningful limit on spending, though it is still the case that a candidate spending the maximum in each state would run up against the overall limit long before all of the primaries were finished.

The Breakdown of FECA

Through the late 1970s and early 1980s, the law worked largely as intended, limiting spending, restricting large contributions, and opening up the system. However, over time, the system began to feel pressures caused by a combination of the growing cost of campaigning and the patchwork shape of the law left behind by *Buckley* v. *Valeo*.

One major problem, as noted earlier, was the increasing cost of campaigning coupled with an unchanging limit on the maximum contributions allowed under the law.[12] The effects of inflation meant that the real purchasing power of a $1,000 contribution in 1976 was approximately $380 as measured by the Consumer Price Index (CPI) in 2000. Thus, candidates needed ever-increasing numbers of contributions just to stay even in purchasing power. Furthermore, the spending limits set for those who accepted public funds became increasingly unrealistic as well. These limits were tied to inflation, so they did rise over time. But the costs associated with campaign activities, particularly regarding television advertising, rose faster than the basic CPI, which was used to set the overall spending limit. In addition, front-loading, as discussed in chapter 2, had the ironic effect of increasing the importance of doing well early, which meant that the state-by-state limits, which in most states were not particularly problematic, became a major issue in the early states, particularly Iowa and New Hampshire. And front-loading also resulted in candidates wrapping up the nomination process earlier, leaving a longer period of time between the actual end of the nomination battle and the formal convention. During this growing interregnum period, candidate spending for those who have accepted public funds is still governed by the nomination limits, putting pressure on the candidates as they attempt to focus their attention on their November opponent.

The response of candidates has been to try to find ways around the FECA regulations. In congressional elections, an increasingly popular way to do this, thanks to the Buckley ruling striking down spending limits and counting a candidate's own money as an expenditure, not a contribution, is to self-finance a campaign, rendering the contribution limits much less relevant. This is more problematic in presidential elections, as such an option means forgoing federal subsidies. But that has not stopped some candidates with the means to do so from exercising this right. Ross Perot, in 1992, refused public funding in the general election, spending over $63 million of his own money on his campaign.[13] The single largest personal contributor to his own presidential election campaigns has been Steve Forbes, who spent approximately $38 million in 1996 and $48 million in 2000 on his unsuccessful efforts to secure the Republican presidential nomination. And in 2004, John Kerry turned down public subsidies in the primaries in order to loan his campaign $6 million late in 2003 when he was struggling to keep up with then-front-runner (in the polls and in money) Howard Dean.

In the nomination phase, candidates also found increasingly creative ways to avoid the state-by-state limits in the early states. In the 2000 New Hampshire Primary, for example, some estimated that as much as 70 percent of Senator McCain's television advertising was credited to other states.[14] This becomes particularly important when a candidate is facing an opponent who has not accepted public funding and thus is not bound by the state-by-state limits. The problems that this created for Bob Dole as a result of the challenge he faced from Steve Forbes in 1992 and the threat of this problem repeating itself in 2000 was one of the reasons given by George W. Bush in 2000 for refusing public subsidies. It also was another reason for John Kerry to refuse matching funds in 2004 once Howard Dean had also announced his intention to do so.

Perhaps the most open response to avoid the state-by-state limits was the decision of Richard Gephardt's campaign in 1988 to simply ignore the limit in Iowa in a last-minute flurry of spending, knowing they would have to pay a fine later. They reasoned that if they did not engage in such spending they would not win the Iowa Caucuses, and that would be the end of their campaign. If they did spend and win, which they did, the fine was a small price to pay.

The overall limit presents a different problem. Theoretically, in a long nomination struggle, a candidate might run out of money before his or her opponent. In practice this has not happened, though it almost was a problem for Walter Mondale in 1984 after he received a surprisingly strong challenge from Gary Hart. And had John McCain done better on Super Tuesday in

2000 and been able to continue his fight against George W. Bush, the only way to do so would have been to violate the spending limit. The same situation would likely have resulted for both Al Gore and Bill Bradley had their battle lasted longer.

More often, this has become a problem for a candidate who has spent his or her money winning the nomination facing an opponent who has resources left from an easier (or nonexistent) nomination battle. Walter Mondale in 1984, George H.W. Bush in 1988, and Bill Clinton in 1992 had to reduce their spending and limit their campaigning in the final weeks before their parties' nominating conventions. Mondale and Bush, in fact, did not limit spending enough and ended up having to pay a penalty for violating the law.

In 1996, however, the Democratic Party found a way to spend money for President Clinton that did not run afoul of spending limits. According to the Supreme Court in *Buckley*, political advertising that did not expressly advocate the election victory or defeat of a specific candidate might not be "campaign spending." According to the Court, if the advertisement did not include words such as "vote for," "elect," "vote against," or "defeat," it was not a campaign expenditure. Rather, this was "issue advocacy." Private groups, then, could spend money on such issue advocacy and began doing so. These ads often name specific candidates but simply ask viewers to "call" the candidate to tell him or her why she or he is right or wrong about some issue. In 1995, the Democratic National Committee (DNC) began running a series of ads promoting President Clinton's issue agenda, paid for with soft money. According to Common Cause, by June 1996, the DNC had spent more than $34 million on issue ads, at least $22 million of which was paid for with soft money, and the Republican National Committee (RNC) had responded with expenditures of over $18 million on behalf of Bob Dole.[15] These expenditures were particularly important for Senator Dole, since he was already at the allowable limit and was not able to do any additional spending on his own. In fact, the party helped maintain his campaign organization by placing forty-four members of his staff on various party payrolls.[16]

These actions in the 1996 campaign were very controversial. But the FEC took no enforcement action against them, giving tacit approval, and this unleashed the floodgates in 2000. Al Gore, who like Dole had run out of funds after spending the limit, was aided by an estimated $25.7 million in expenditures by the DNC during the interregnum. And the RNC spent an estimated $22.3 million in support of George W. Bush in spite of the fact that his refusal of public subsidies and large war chest meant that he had plenty of money of his own to spend.[17]

Furthermore, the parties and other groups continued their soft-money issue advocacy advertising into the general election, undermining the general election limits in spite of having both candidates accept the full public subsidy. According to the Brennan Center, the 2000 campaign was the first election under FECA where parties and groups spent more on political advertising in the presidential campaign than the candidates did.[18] As table 3-2 shows, the parties spent $12.7 million more than the candidates in the seventy-five largest media markets in the United States.

TABLE 3-2: Television Advertising in 75 Largest Media Markets, 2000 Presidential Election

Advertising For Bush	Advertising For Gore
Bush Campaign 39.2	Gore Campaign 27.9
Republican Party 44.7	Democratic Party 35.1
Political Groups 2.1	Political Groups 14.0
Total: 86.0	Total: 77.0

Source: Brennan Center for Justice figures, as reported in Corrado, "Financing the 2000 Presidential General Election," 94.
Figures are millions of dollars.

This breakdown of the FECA rules and regulations was not limited to the presidential campaign. In fact, in many ways the growth of soft money, issue advocacy, and self-financed candidates, among other problems, created more issues for congressional campaigns than they did at the presidential level, where the public subsidy system supplemented the private finance regime of FECA.[19] And this breakdown led to passage of the Bipartisan Campaign Reform Act (BCRA). But while the law does address the soft money/issue advocacy issue, it does little to solve the underlying problems of the presidential finance system.

The Bipartisan Campaign Reform Act

The Bipartisan Campaign Reform Act was designed to reestablish the system set up by the FECA, a system designed to encourage relatively small contributions (to prevent any single contributor or group from having "too much" influence), a level playing field, and transparency.[20] The bill was signed into law by President Bush on March 27, 2002, and went into effect on November 6, 2002, the day after the mid-term elections.[21] The major focus of the reform was on controlling or eliminating "soft-money" and "issue-advocacy" spending that undermined the controls exercised over "hard-money" fundraising and expenditures by political campaigns. As applied to presidential elections, there were four aspects of BCRA that were particularly relevant.

First, the contribution limit was raised from $1,000 to $2,000 per election and was, for the future, indexed for inflation. This makes it easier for candidates to raise hard money for their campaigns.

Second, political parties are prohibited from spending soft money on behalf of presidential candidates. Spending by parties on activities that had been financed with soft money must now be financed with hard-money dollars subject to contribution limits and full disclosure. The effect of this is felt most strongly in the interregnum period when the candidates have wrapped up the nomination but have not yet officially been designated at the convention, a time when candidates have often been "out of money." But it also limits party activity in the general election.[22]

Third, groups are prohibited from running "issue advocacy" ads that name a candidate for federal office within thirty days of a primary election or sixty days of a general election. Inside those thirty- or sixty-day windows, only "hard-money" independent expenditures are permitted. This means that groups supporting a candidate can still spend unlimited soft money in the interregnum period (which, as we will see, has led to some of the remaining controversy over the bill) but must stop such activities in the final two months of the campaign.

Finally, there is the impact of changes that were not made. BCRA raised the individual contribution limit. But it did not increase or index the $250 ceiling for public matching funds in the primaries. Thus, the relative usefulness of matching funds declines even more precipitously. The maximum match prior to 2004 was one-fourth of the maximum contribution allowed. That is now one-eighth and will continue to decline over time. Similarly, the formula for expenditure limits tied to public financing has not been adjusted. This makes it likely that candidates who accept public funds will reach their limit more quickly.

The law was immediately challenged in court. This was, of course, not a surprise, and the law itself was written to allow for expedited review. On December 10, 2003, the Supreme Court, in the case of *McConnell* v. *Federal Election Commission* (124 S. Ct. 619, 657, 2003), upheld nearly all elements of the law. The contribution limits, bans on soft money, and limits on issue advocacy were all found to be constitutional.[23] In fact, supporters of the law found little in the decision to complain about.[24] Don Simon, the general counsel for Common Cause, called it a "striking vindication for the work of Common Cause" and "a sweeping victory for BCRA, and for the compelling public importance of efforts to regulate money in the political process in order to deter both corruption and the appearance of corruption."[25]

The net result of all of this, however, is that the underlying problems of presidential campaign finance have been exacerbated, even if some of the difficulties—such as the ease of large contributors to circumvent contribution limits—have been ameliorated. In fact, the 2004 election demonstrated the growing incentive that candidates have to refuse public funding and the spending limits that go with them, leading to even longer periods of high-volume political advertising, which the public finds so alienating.

The Problems with BCRA

In looking at the impact of BCRA, it is important to remember that presidential campaign finance faced a different set of problems than those faced in restructuring other federal elections. In presidential campaign finance, the public funding system was designed to limit the influence of private contributors and to limit spending, creating a system where money mattered less in determining the strategy of the candidates and the outcome of the election. BCRA does limit the direct influence of large contributors. The ban on party soft money and limits on issue-advocacy spending by groups makes campaigns and parties much more dependent on smaller contributions. While both candidates still raised the bulk of their money in contributions of over $1,000, they both raised much more from smaller contributions than any previous presidential campaigns.[26] And the parties also vastly expanded their donor bases.[27] The percentage of contributions to presidential candidates coming from small contributions jumped on the Republican side from 16 percent in 2000 to 31 percent in 2004, while for the Democrats the percentage jumped from 20 percent to 37 percent.[28] This greater reliance on more small contributions is a move in the right direction.

However, BCRA continued—and in fact made stronger—the growing incentive for candidates to opt out of the public funding system. By moving toward greater reliance on private funding, this has the effect of eliminating the spending caps that go along with the public funds, requiring candidates to spend more time raising money and leading to much greater spending during the campaign, most of which still goes into flooding the airwaves with political advertisements.

BCRA exacerbates this problem in two ways. First, it did not adjust the match of funds in the nomination phase to take into account either the impact of inflation on dollar-based limits or the higher individual contribution limit that comes with BCRA. Thus, through the 2000 election, federal matching funds matched individual contributions worth one-quarter of the individual contribution limit. So a contribution of $250 that was matched to give the candidate $500 in total was worth one-half of the maximum individual contribution of $1,000. In 2004 it was only worth one-quarter of the $2,000 maximum contribution. And since that maximum is now pegged to inflation, the value of the match, in relative terms, will continue to decline.

Second, the spending limits that go along with accepting the matching funds were not raised, either. This, as we have seen, is particularly problematic in the small, early states such as Iowa and New Hampshire, where the state-by-state limits do not reflect the importance of the states in the electoral calendar, and in the interregnum period where candidates run the risk of being vastly outspent by an opponent who was not forced to spend as much money in the nomination struggle or who did not accept public funds. In fact, part of President Bush's strategy for 2004 was to unleash a torrent of spending after the Democratic candidate was clear. The desire to avoid such a problem led Howard Dean, and then John Kerry, to opt out of public funds as well. Thus, the 2004 election witnessed unprecedented campaign spending by both campaigns in the period where the nominees were clear, but the conventions had not yet been held. By the end of July 2004, John Kerry had spent $185 million, compared to the $44 million Al Gore had spent in 2000 with the limitations he had because of the acceptance of public funding. More tellingly, George Bush, with no limitations in either year, had spent $209 million in 2004, compared to $97 million in 2000. And this also meant that both candidates spent a great deal of time during this period raising money, as by the end of July 2004 they had raised 88 percent more money than had been raised at a comparable time in 2000.[29] Clearly, in the future, the incentive to opt out of public funding, with its built-in limits, will continue to grow.

Furthermore, this temptation to opt out of public funding is even greater because of the spread of fundraising techniques pioneered in the 2000 campaign by President Bush and the 2004 campaign by Howard Dean. The Bush campaigns in 2000 and 2004 were able to raise enormous sums of money by creating a system where individuals pledge to raise money for the campaign and are rewarded for reaching particular levels of contributions. In the Bush campaign, there were three levels: Pioneers, Rangers, and Mavericks. An individual who reached one of these levels was rewarded with public recognition (the names of all people in each category were listed on the Bush campaign website), invitations to events, "privileged" campaign information, and other such perks. Critics of the role of money in politics expressed concern that more was being gained by these individuals than this public recognition and seemingly trivial perks.[30] Senator Kerry copied this technique in 2004 by listing on his website (without any catchy names for the categories) individuals who raised between $50,000 and $100,000, and those who raised over $100,000.[31]

Similarly, Howard Dean's campaign was able to raise enormous sums of money via the Internet by applying fundraising techniques familiar to those who watch telethon fundraising efforts. Candidates have been using the Internet to raise funds since the technology made it easy and safe. What Dean did, however, was to create a series of short-term goals to motivate people to contribute. He would let his supporters know that he needed to raise a particular amount by a certain date. The website would proclaim, for example, that "we need another $5 million by Friday to set a record for the month." Or that "we need $2 million by Tuesday to fight the negative ads our opponents are planning." And the website would track progress toward the goal, creating both a sense of urgency and a sense of accomplishment (as goal after goal was met). And, of course, Dean's success spurred other candidates to copy this type of appeal.

The ability of candidates to use these techniques to raise larger and larger sums of privately contributed funds makes it even easier for candidates to opt out of the public finance scheme. And while there may be some benefits to the broadening base of contributors that emerge, particularly with the widespread use of the Internet (Howard Dean raised 59 percent of his money, over $30 million, in contributions of $200 or less),[32] the saturation advertising that it allows overwhelms the public, alienating it further from the system.

The other issue raised by BCRA is the role of so-called 527 groups (named for the section of the IRS code under which they are organized). 527s are non-profit groups that have as their principal purpose the influencing of elections. These groups can engage in any activity they want to as long as they use "hard money" (that is, money subject to the contribution limits of

FECA/BCRA). But these groups also can have soft-money accounts, which would allow for unlimited individual, corporate, or union contributions that can be used for activities such as nonpartisan mobilization efforts. The questions that the FEC needed to address, since the answers were not entirely clear from either the law or the Supreme Court's decision in *McConnell* v. *FEC*, was whether these soft-money funds could be used in political ads that explicitly promote, support, attack, or oppose a candidate for federal office outside of the thirty-day (in the primaries) or sixty-day (in the general election) window and whether such soft money could be used in partisan voter mobilization drives. This was a particularly divisive issue, as many long-time supporters of campaign finance reform wanted very strict regulations concerning the use of soft money by 527s, while other supporters of reform were concerned that strict regulations would be an infringement on the free-speech rights of these groups or would be particularly problematic for the Democrats, as they have historically relied more heavily on soft money than the Republicans, and many supporters of the party had been quick to set up 527s in anticipation of passage of BCRA.[33]

The FEC moved through the rule process as the 2004 campaign proceeded, finally refusing, on May 14, to impose further restrictions on 527 groups, allowing them to continue to raise soft money as they had in the past.[34] This action led to a rush by Republicans to set up their own 527s and for Democrats to redouble their activities.[35] And while these 527s did not completely replace all of the party soft money that BCRA eliminated, they did provide an avenue for much of that money to find its way into the campaign.[36] Reformers immediately began to call for further regulation of 527s. Senators McCain and Feingold, the prime movers of BCRA, issued a joint press release that said, in part: "The commission has failed to close a loophole that dangerously undermines the purpose of the federal campaign finance laws.... As a result, a flood of soft money will enter the system which will violate the letter and the spirit of the law."[37] But as we shall see in chapter 6, patchwork reforms involving only 527s are unlikely to do much good, as groups will simply shift their money to other avenues that would still be available. For now, we simply need to note that the burst of activity channeled through 527s gave citizens the sense that their concerns about the role of money in the election process had not been addressed by BCRA.

Conclusion

In spite of the efforts of reformers in passing BCRA, money continues—in the eyes of the public—to have a corrosive effect on the presidential election system. The vast amounts of money raised and spent lead citizens to believe that the system is not fair to those without access to enormous amounts of money and create a system where saturation political advertising, much of it negative, causes people to see the system as out of control. Part of this problem is actually made worse by BCRA, as it encourages candidates to opt out of the public funding system and the spending limits that they impose. If a way could be found to continue the high density of small contributions that were evident in the Dean campaign without also encouraging the use of "Pioneers" and other individuals with access to many potential contributors, and to curb seemingly unlimited amounts of money, the public might begin to develop more faith in the system. And reformers have made proposals to try to deal with these problems in the system. Senators McCain and Feingold and Representatives Shays and Meehan, the prime sponsors of BCRA, for example, introduced a bill in 2003 (before the impact of BCRA on the 2004 election was at all clear) that was scheduled to begin with the 2008 election and would, among other things: (1) increase the size of the public match of contributions from the current 1:1 ratio to a 4:1 ratio (that is, for a $250 contribution, the candidate would receive a $1,000 match); (2) require candidates to opt in or out of public funding for both the nomination and general election together, not as separate decisions as with the current law; and (3) provide greater public funds for candidates running against opponents who opt out of public funding and spend substantially more than the public funds limit would normally allow.[38]

Other reform groups have made similar proposals.[39] And we will take a closer look in chapter 6 at the issue of changes to help the system. But we also need to recognize that the debilitating impact of money is exacerbated by changes in technology and campaigning that make it easier for candidates to target their spending to particular segments of the population. This is most clearly seen in the way that the impact of the rules of the Electoral College have, over time, led to a situation of feast or famine for the public, alienating much of it from the process, even if for different reasons depending upon the state in which one lives, as it impacts candidate strategy and tactics throughout the campaign. It is to the Electoral College and these broader changes that we now turn.

Notes

1 These figures come from the American National Election Study and can be found at their website at www.umich.edu/~nes/nesguide/toptable/tab5b_3.htm.

2 For more comprehensive histories of campaign finance see Sorauf, Frank, *Money in American Elections* (Glenview, IL: Scott Foresman, 1988); Alexander, Herbert, *Financing Politics: Money, Elections and Political Reform* (Washington, DC: Congressional Quarterly, 1984); Corrado, Anthony, *Paying for Presidents* (New York: Twentieth Century Fund Press, 1993); Gierzynski, Anthony, *Money Rules: Financing Elections in America* (Boulder, CO: Westview Press, 2000); and ch. two of Wayne, Stephen, *The Road to the White House 2004* (Belmont, CA: Thompson/Wadsworth, 2004).

3 Prior to adoption of the Australian ballot, party workers could hand a preprinted ballot to the voter and watch him—and in those days it was him! —put it in the ballot box, insuring that only those who actually voted for the party were paid.

4 These figures come from Alexander, *Financing Politics*.

5 The break-in at Democratic Party headquarters at the Watergate apartment complex by operatives of the Nixon campaign gave name to a variety of activities carried out by the president and his campaign, some of which were directly related to campaign finance. For example, the campaign's deputy finance director, Jeb MacGruder, was convicted of soliciting illegal corporate campaign contributions, and twenty-one corporate executives pled guilty to making illegal contributions from corporate treasuries.

6 For more comprehensive discussions of the law, see the references in note 2 above. Also, see Corrado, Anthony, *Campaign Finance Reform: Beyond the Basics* (New York: Century Foundation Press, 2000); Green, John, and Bigelow, Nathan, "The 2000 Presidential Nominations: The Costs of Innovation," in Magleby, David, ed., *Financing the 2000 Election* (Washington, DC: Brookings Institution Press, 2002); and Corrado, Anthony, "Financing the 2000 Elections," in Pomper, Gerald, ed., *The Election of 2000* (New York: Chatham House, 2001).

7 The Campaign Finance Institute can be found at cfinst.org, while the Center for Responsive Politics is at opensecrets.org. At the CRP's website one can search for information by campaign or look up groups and individuals and see to whom they are giving money. These are just two of the sites devoted to the influence of money on elections. There are many others.

8 Which meant $2,000 in practice, since the primary election was treated as a separate election from the general election.

9 Unions and corporations, not allowed to spend their own funds on campaigns, were allowed to set up separate PACs, which raised money from members and employees for express political purposes. The unions and corporations are allowed to pay for overhead expenses from their treasuries. But "political" expenditures must come from the money raised explicitly for that purpose. There are also PACs set up by ideological organizations and by political leaders.

10 The actual figure was $74.62 million.

11 All of the figures for 2004 in this section come from the estimates made by the Federal Election Commission, as reported in Kort, Amy, "Estimated Presidential Spending Lim-

its," in The Federal Election Commission, *The Record* 29, no. 11, November 2003. They also can be found at http://www.fec.gov/pages/brochures/pubfund_limits_2004. shtml.

12 For more complete accounts of the breakdown of FECA in presidential elections see Corrado, Anthony, and Gouvea, Heitor, "Financing Presidential Nominations under the BCRA," in Mayer, William, ed., *The Making of the Presidential Candidates 2004* (Lanham, MD: Rowman & Littlefield, 2004); Green, John, and Corrado, Anthony, "The Impact of BCRA on Presidential Campaign Finance," in Malbin, Michael, ed., *Life After Reform: When the Bipartisan Campaign Reform Act Meets Politics* (Lanham, MD: Rowman & Littlefield, 2003); and Wayne, *The Road to the White House 2004*.

13 In 1996, Perot did accept the public funds in the general election, limiting himself to $50,000, though he did spend more than $8 million of his own money on the nomination campaign, some of which was spent to get the Reform Party on the ballot in all fifty states.

14 See Fowler, Linda; Spiliotes, Constantine; and Vavreck, Linda, "The Role of Issue Advocacy in the New Hampshire Primary," in Magleby, David, ed., *Getting Inside the Outside Campaign* (Provo, UT: Brigham Young University, Center for the Study of Elections and Democracy, 2000). In the same volume, also see Sanders, Arthur, and Redlawsk, David, "Money and the Iowa Caucuses."

15 Common Cause, "Statement of Common Cause President Ann McBride at News Conference Asking for Independent Counsel to Investigate Campaign Finance Activities of Clinton, Dole Campaigns," Press Release, 9 October 1996.

16 Corrado and Gouvea, "Financing Presidential Nominations Under the BCRA," 66.

17 These estimates are reported in Corrado and Gouvea, "Financing Presidential Nominations Under the BCRA," and come from Corrado, Anthony; Barclay, Sarah; and Gouvea, Henry, "The Parties Take the Lead: Political Parties and the Financing of the 2000 Presidential Election," in Green, John, and Farmer, Rick, eds., *The State of the Parties*, 4th ed. (Lanham, MD: Rowman & Littlefield, 2003).

18 Brennan Center for Justice, "2000 Presidential Race First in Modern History Where Political Parties Spend More on TV Ads Than Candidates," Press Release, New York, 11 December 2000. These figures can also be found in Corrado, "Financing the 2000 Presidential Elections."

19 The problems of campaign finance in congressional elections are beyond the scope of this chapter. For good summaries see Magleby, *Financing the 2000 Election*; Malbin, *Life After Reform*; Herrnson, Paul, *Congressional Elections: Campaigning at Home and in Washington*, 4th ed. (Washington, DC: CQ Press, 2004); and Jacobson, Gary, *The Politics of Congressional Elections*, 6th ed. (New York: Longman, 2004).

20 For good summaries of BCRA, especially how it relates to presidential campaign finance, see Malbin, *Life After Reform*; Corrado and Gouvea, "Financing Presidential Nominations under the BCRA"; and Common Cause, *A Reporter's Guide to Money in Politics: Campaign 2004* (Washington, DC: Common Cause), 25 November 2003.

21 One provision of the law, increased contribution limits, did not go into effect until 1 January 2003.

22 There also was a provision in the law that forced parties to choose between independent and coordinated expenditures. Coordinated expenditures, where the party consults with

the candidate on strategy, message, and other factors, are limited, while independent expenditures are not. But with independent expenditures, party officials are prohibited from working with the candidate. This provision of the law, however, was struck down by the Supreme Court.

23 The case can be found on-line at a257.g.akamaitech.net/7/257/2422/10dec20031140/ www.supremecourtus.gov/opinions/03pdf/02-1674.pdf.

24 For analyses of the decision, see Mann, Thomas, and Ornstein, Norman, "Separating Myth from Reality in McConnell v. FEC," *Election Law Journal*, March 2002; and Simon, Don, *McConnell v. FEC: BCRA Analysis*, found at www.commoncause.org/news /default.cfm?ArtID=261. 12 December 2003.

25 Simon, Don, *McConnell v. FEC*, An Analysis of the Case in an Open Letter to the Common Cause Community, 11 December 2003, available to download as a PDF file at www.commoncause.org/atf/cf/%7BFB3C17E2-CDD1-4DF692BEBD4429893665%7DD JS-Supreme%20Court%20Analysis.pdf; 8.

26 To give one example, in just one month, March 2004, President Bush raised 39 percent of his money, over $10 million in contributions of under $200. This would have set a new record for money raised in such small amounts, except that John Kerry raised close to $16 million in such small contributions that month as well. See Weissman, Steve, "CFI Analysis of the Presidential Candidates' Financial Reports Filed April 20: Bush and Kerry Emphasized Small Contributions," available at www.cfinst.org/pr/042202.html.

27 For a comprehensive look at small donors in the 2004 campaign, see the study by the Institute for Politics, Democracy and the Internet, *Small Donors and Online Giving* (Washington, DC: George Washington University, 2006).

28 Ibid., 4.

29 Weissman, Stephen, "CFI Analysis of the Presidential Candidates' Financial Reports Filed August 20, 2004," Campaign Finance Institute Press Release, 25 August 2004, available at http://www.cfinst.org/pr/082504.html. The figures come from table 1, which can be downloaded from that site.

30 See, for example, Common Cause, "Prospecting for Access: How the Bush Pioneers Shaped Public Policy," found at www.commoncause.org/justwatch, October 2003. This report details the amount of money raised by a number of Bush Pioneers in 2000 and the subsequent public policy decisions made by the Bush Administration that were of benefit to these individuals and their businesses. This information can also be found at the website WhiteHouseforsale.org.

31 Similarly both Wesley Clark and Howard Dean publicly recognized individuals who had raised substantial sums of money for their campaigns, with both of them calling these people "Rain Makers."

32 Only Dennis Kucinich, who raised over two-thirds of his money in such small contributions, raised a higher percentage of his funds from small contributions. See Weissman, Steven "CFI Analysis of Presidential Candidates Financial Reports Filed June 20," table 3, available at http://www.cfinst.org/pr/063004.html.

33 For an example of those wanting strict regulations, see Wertheimer, Fred, "FEC Rulemaking Proceeding Will Determine Whether FEC Recreates Soft Money System in the 2004 Federal Elections," A Report for Democracy 21, found at the Democracy 21 web-

site, wwwldemocracy21.org. For an example of reform groups concerned with overly strict regulations, see the statement released by Common Cause, "Common Cause and Brennan Center File Comments with FEC Regarding 527 Advisory Opinion," and "Common Cause submits FEC comments on 527s" both at the Common Cause website, www.commoncause.org.

34 Justice, Glenn, "The 2004 Campaign: Campaign Finance; F.E.C. Declines to Curb Independent Fund-Raisers," *The New York Times*, 14 May 2004, A18.

35 Justice, Glenn, "The 2004 Campaign: Campaign Finance; Republicans Rush to Form New Finance Groups," *The New York Times*, 29 May 2004, A1.

36 Weissman, Stephen, and Hassan, Ruth, "BCRA and the 527 Groups," in Malbin, Michael, ed., *The Election After Reform* (Lanham, MD: Rowman & Littlefield, 2006), ch. 5.

37 Quoted in Justice, "The 2004 Campaign: Campaign Finance; F.E.C. Declines to Curb Independent Fund-Raisers," A18.

38 See Democracy 21, "Presidential Funding Act of 2003 Bill Summary," 21 November 2003, found at http://www.democracy21.org/index.asp?Type=B_PR&SEC={FD714569-5FB3-45D6-82D4-A3098EE124BA}&DE={00F9A0CF-5949-4D97-847CA376348353EA}.

39 See, for example, the comprehensive proposal from the Campaign Finance Institute Task Force on Presidential Nomination Financing, *Participation, Competition, Engagement: How to Revive and Improve Public Funding for Presidential Nomination Politics* (Washington, DC: Campaign Finance Institute, 2003).

CHAPTER 4

The Electoral College

In July 1960, when he formally accepted the Republican nomination for president, Vice-President Richard Nixon told the convention and a national television audience that he was going to "carry this campaign into every one of the fifty states."[1] Nixon argued that it was going to be a very close election and that the votes of every state might count.[2] Even at that time it was a controversial promise, especially after a two-week illness kept the vice-president in the hospital, forcing him to squeeze his campaign into an even shorter time frame. But today, no candidate would ever make such a promise or such a claim, and, in fact, no candidate since Nixon has visited all fifty states. Candidates today focus their energy in a much more targeted way, attempting to win not the most votes, though that is a nice thing to do, but the 270 electoral votes it takes to win the presidency. The Electoral College, then, is central to campaign strategy and the allocation of campaign resources. At one level that has always been true, for we have always elected the president by this method and not by the direct votes of citizens. But changes in technology have made it easier for candidates to figure out how to target that Electoral College majority and to reach that audience without "wasting" resources in other areas. And this, in turn, leads to a situation much like that which occurs in the nomination process: In some places citizens are oversaturated with campaign ads, candidate appearances, and efforts, while in most places, the campaign hardly exists, a combination that leaves no one satisfied. In this chapter we will take a look at the Electoral College, how it structures the campaign, and why its impact is greater now than it has ever been.

The Electoral College

The rules of the Electoral College are the result of the compromises made by the delegates to the Constitutional Convention, one important and a second minor amendment to the U.S. Constitution, and three crucial changes in practice that those who wrote the original rules did not anticipate.

There was a great deal of debate over the method that should be used to choose the chief executive.[3] Some wanted the president chosen by Congress. Others wanted the people to elect the president directly. But the convention decided on a method of selection by an intermediate group of electors. It was a compromise that had something for everyone, but that completely satisfied no one. John Roche, in his well-known defense of the work of the convention, stated that it was "neither an exercise in applied Platonism nor an experiment in indirect government based on elitist distrust of the masses. It was merely a jerry-rigged improvisation which has subsequently been endowed with a high theoretical content."[4]

Under the system adopted by the Constitution, each state would be entitled to an electoral vote total equal to its representation in Congress, and it would take a majority of the electoral vote to be chosen president. Were no one to receive a majority vote, the House of Representatives would choose the president from the top five finishers in the Electoral College, but voting in the House would be by state delegation, each state receiving a single vote and a majority of states needed to win. This satisfied both the big states and the small states. The founders expected that, except in unusual circumstances, different candidates for president would be championed in different states. The bigger states would have an advantage in the initial electoral vote count, in effect dominating the top five positions, but the method of voting in the House would give the small states power over which person emerged the winner from that selection process. The method of selection of the electors was left to the states, which satisfied both those who wanted the public involved (as states could allow the people to choose the electors), and those who did not trust the people (since states could leave that selection process in the state legislature, and even if they did not, there was another layer or two—depending upon whether or not the election went to the House—between the people's votes and the actual selection of the president). The delegates to the convention all assumed—correctly, as it turned out—that whatever selection method they chose, George Washington would be the first president. This assumption probably muted some of the potential discord over the method settled on, as there was little underlying struggle to help any particular person increase his chances of election.

So on Election Day, when we go into the voting booth, we are not actually voting for president. We are voting for a group of electors pledged to support the candidate we prefer. And that is one of the informal changes that altered the nature of the Electoral College. It has become more democratic. In the early years of the nation, most electors were chosen by the state legislatures, though states often changed their rules. Massachusetts changed its rules seven times in the first ten national elections.[5] But the clear trend was to move from a system of legislative choice to one of popular choice. By 1824, popular election of electors was the rule in all but six states. After 1832, South Carolina was the only state to deny citizens direct selection of electors, a situation that was the case until 1860. Since the Civil War, there have only been two instances when states had their legislatures choose the electors, Florida in 1868 and Colorado in 1876.[6] Thus, the Electoral College has become a much more democratically oriented institution.

The second important informal change in the process was the development of strong national political parties. These national political parties, first the Jeffersonian Republicans (who later evolved into the contemporary Democratic Party) and then the Federalists and later the Whigs, would put forth candidates for the electors (and, later, the public) to choose. Thus, rather than the Electoral College serving as a kind of nominating arena presenting choices for the House to vote upon, the parties became the nominating arena, and the Electoral College became the final arbiter, choosing the president. The selection of the president has gone to the House only twice, the first time in 1800 because of a quirk in the rules that we will look at in a moment. The second time was in 1824, when the House of Representatives chose John Quincy Adams as president, defeating the candidate with the most popular votes (at least in those states that chose electors by popular votes), Andrew Jackson. This helped to spur the movement toward popular election of electors that was noted above.

This move to national political parties as the method of nomination also had the effect of turning the electors into "bound" delegates rather then the free agents the founders envisioned. Political parties would now choose the electors. The exact method varies from state to state.[7] Most require the parties to nominate the electors by party convention, but there is much variation in the specifics, and in California, state law actually provides different rules for Democrats and Republicans. The bottom line, however, is the same. Electors are chosen because of their loyalty to the party and are expected to vote for the party's candidate should they be elected. Under the Constitution, electors were intended to be free agents using their judgment to help select a president. But parties and the public expect electors to carry out their will, and that is almost always the case. Since the founding of the Electoral College, there have been only 156 faithless electors. Seventy-five of those have involved only the vice-presidential selection, leaving eighty-one truly faithless presidential electors. However, sixty-three of those were Democratic electors pledged to vote for Horace Greeley in 1872. But Greeley had died between the general election and the day on which the electors voted, so it is not clear how "faithless" these electors actually were. This, then, leaves only eighteen truly faithless electors in presidential elections, only eight of whom came after 1832, and none of them made any difference in the outcome of an election. Thus, while some may be concerned with the potential problem such electors might cause, in practice the shift to national political parties as the nomination mechanism has led to bound electors who support their party's candidate.[8]

The third important change—popular selection and national political parties being the first two—was a practical political choice made by the states, the adoption of winner-take-all-electors elections. Under this unit rule, whichever party won the state would win all of the state's electors. Many of the nation's early leaders, including Jefferson, Madison, Hamilton, Andrew Jackson, and John Quincy Adams, preferred a district system where each congressional district in the state would choose a single elector, and two "bonus" electors would be given to the person who carried the entire state.[9]

But the district plan was never particularly popular at the state level. The pressure to use a unit system came from two sources. First was internal political dealings in the various states. Whichever party controlled the legislature had incentive to maximize its power by adopting a unit rule. And second, once other states began adopting the unit rule, there was external pressure to do so in order to keep the influence of the state at its peak. The district system was, therefore, never particularly popular in spite of the desire of many of those who designed the Electoral College. (Madison wrote in 1823 that "the district system was mostly, if not exclusively, in view when the Constitution was framed and adopted."[10]) The use of the district system reached its peak in 1820 when six states used it, but it had disappeared by 1836. Maine resurrected it in 1969 for use beginning in 1972, and Nebraska adopted it beginning in 1992. But those two states and their nine electoral votes (four for Maine, five for Nebraska) are the only states employing this system.

There were also two formal constitutional changes to the Electoral College. One was the relatively minor change of providing three electoral votes to the citizens of the District of Columbia in the Twenty-Third Amendment, ratified in 1961. But the other, provided by the Twelfth Amendment, ratified in 1804, was more significant. Under the original Constitution, each elector named two people on his ballot. (And at the time of this rule, it always was "his"!) The person finishing first was to become president. The person with the second most votes, whether or not it was also a majority, would be vice-president. That was how President John Adams ended up with his political rival, Thomas Jefferson, as his vice-president.

The development of national political parties led to the need to change this rule. In 1800, all of the Jeffersonian electors cast their votes for Thomas Jefferson and Aaron Burr. Everyone knew that Jefferson was supposed to be the president, but the choice fell to the House.[11] All of the Republican members of the House voted for Jefferson, but there was a Federalist majority in the House, and many of them did not want to see their bitter political rival Jefferson elected, so they supported Burr. And had Burr been willing to promise to "govern as a Federalist," he might have won. But he was not willing to make such a promise, and some Federalists, most notably his bitter New York political rival, Alexander Hamilton, threw their support to Jefferson. This led to a deadlock in the House that did not end until the thirty-sixth ballot, when Jefferson was finally chosen president. Burr's anger with Hamilton over this never dissipated, and after Hamilton worked to defeat him yet again in his unsuccessful run for governor of New York, Burr shot and killed Hamilton in a duel on July 11, 1804.

The events of 1800 made it clear that changes were needed, and that led to passage of the Twelfth Amendment. Under this amendment, electors vote separately for president and vice-president, majorities being needed for both. If a presidential election were thrown into the House, the House would, using the same one-vote-per-state method provided for in the original Constitution, choose the president from the top three—not five—finishers in the Electoral College. And in the event that no one had a majority of the vice-presidential vote, the Senate would choose the vice-president from the top two finishers. Finally, because there was still concern that this process would be dominated by large states, not national political parties, it was stipulated that no elector could vote for both a president and vice-president who came from their state. That provision caused Dick Cheney to move out of Texas and back to Wyoming prior to the 2000 election.[12]

We have a system, then, where a presidential election is not a single nationwide election, but fifty separate statewide elections, plus an additional election in the District of Columbia and in five congressional districts in Nebraska and Maine. That shapes both candidate strategy and the way citizens respond to their electoral environment in ways that undermine democracy. And it is to that impact that we now turn.

The Impact of the Electoral College

From a democratic perspective, the major problem with the Electoral College is that the person with the most votes does not necessarily win the election. That problem was brought home to many in 2000, when Al Gore's popular-vote majority did not lead to his election as president, as George W. Bush was able to win a majority in the Electoral College. That result was almost reversed in 2004, when John Kerry came within 65,000 votes in Ohio of capturing the electoral vote while losing the popular vote by over 3 million votes. Ironically, the heated and prolonged controversy over the outcome in Florida in 2000, a controversy that only mattered because of the closeness of the Electoral College vote, took much public attention away from the fact that Vice-President Gore had, in fact, won the popular vote.[13] The fact that the candidate who could more legitimately claim to be "the people's choice" was not the winner took a backseat to the legal and public-relations battle over the recount in Florida. As in 1884, when popular-vote winner Grover Cleveland lost the Electoral College vote to Benjamin Harrison, and in 1876 when Electoral College winner Rutherford B. Hayes almost certainly had fewer popular votes than Samuel Tilden,[14] the election of 2000 produced a result where the person with the most votes did not win.[15] In terms of such split outcomes, mention should also be made of 1960. According to published final popular-vote tallies, John Kennedy won a very narrow margin of victory over Richard Nixon in the popular vote. But the ballot in Alabama listed the names of Electoral College delegates, not the presidential candidates, and six of the eleven Democratic delegates were opposed to the national party and Senator Kennedy because of his (and the national party's) stand on civil rights. Thus, it is difficult to know exactly how many popular votes Kennedy actually received in Alabama. *Congressional Quarterly* developed two methods to count the Alabama vote. The one they used gave Kennedy a 112,827-vote plurality in Alabama, and a national popular-vote victory. Had they used the other method, however, they would have given Nixon a popular vote lead in both Alabama and the nation.[16] Thus, in its most direct challenge to democratic ideals, the Electoral College has given us presidents who did not "win" the election.

This problem is exacerbated by the fact that the number of electoral votes a state receives is a function of the most recent census. It is determined in advance and thus is completely unrelated to voter turnout. California gets more electoral votes than any other state no matter what the turnout is. Theoretically, an earthquake could wipe out three-quarters of California's population, but until the next census, California would still be the state with the most electoral votes. But to give a more concrete example, according to the 1990 census, Minnesota received ten electoral votes, and Tennessee received eleven. In the 2000 election, slightly fewer than 2.1 million people voted in Tennessee for those eleven electoral votes. But in Minnesota over 2.4 million people voted for only ten electoral votes. In fact, more people voted in Minnesota than in three states awarded more electoral votes, the other two being Missouri, with eleven electoral votes and 2.3 million people voting, and Indiana, with twelve electoral votes but only 2.2 million voting.[17]

Campaigns, then, will target states based on how many electoral votes they offer and how competitive they are likely to be. A campaign will draw up a list of three groups of states: those they feel sure to win, those they feel sure to lose, and those that are up for grabs. Only those in the final category are given the full attention of the campaign. And in that group, because of the winner-take-all system within the states, the larger states are more important than the smaller ones. Occasionally the two campaigns will differ on which states are competitive, but the lists tend to overlap. And it is easy to figure out which states each side is targeting by watching where the candidates go and where they spend money on television advertising. And with constant monitoring and polling, the campaigns can adjust and refocus their strategies if a competitive state seems to be moving safely into the group of states supporting one of the candidates, or if one of the safe states seems to have become competitive. In 2004 both campaigns started with a list of eighteen states they thought would be competitive. This list included the sixteen states that were decided by less than six percentage points in 2000: Arkansas, Florida, Iowa, Maine, Michigan, Minnesota, Missouri, Nevada, New Hampshire, New Mexico, Ohio, Oregon, Pennsylvania, Tennessee, Washington, and Wisconsin. In addition there were two states, Arizona and West Virginia, that were not as close in 2000 but were seen by both sides as being competitive in 2004. And there were four states where one side or the other thought they might be able to move into the competitive category: Delaware and New Jersey for the Bush campaign, Colorado and Louisiana for the Kerry campaign.[18] A citizen who did not live in those twenty-two states was never the target of either campaign.

Over the course of the campaign, the targeting shifted substantially, and by the fall it was clear to both sides that nine states were actually in play: Florida, Iowa, Michigan, Minnesota, New Hampshire, New Mexico, Ohio, Pennsylvania, and Wisconsin, and that is where the bulk of the campaign took place. Citizens inside those nine states were saturated with visits from the candidates, campaign advertising, and on-the-ground personal campaigning. Those who lived in states that appeared on the original lists of targeted states started off with some campaign activity (and since some infrastructure was created, some of that activity continued),[19] while those in states that were never the target of either campaign saw little or no campaign activity.[20] This can be seen in three different ways. First, there is the number of visits that candidates (presidential and vice-presidential) made to each state. Table 4-1 lists the number of Democratic and Republican presidential candidate visits to each of the nine fully targeted states.

TABLE 4-1: Presidential Visits by State

	Repub. Visits	Dem. Visits	Tot. Visits
Ohio	21	32	53
Florida	16	27	43
Wisconsin	14	20	34
Pennsylvania	16	16	32
Iowa	15	15	30
Michigan	10	8	18
Minnesota	10	8	18
New Mexico	9	6	15
New Hampshire	4	6	10
Partially Targeted (14)	33	30	63
Non-Targeted (28)	10	11	21

Figures are from *The New York Times* and abcnews.com reported by Pomper, Gerald, "The Presidential Campaign," in Nelson, Michael, *The Elections of 2004*, table 3-5, p. 55.
The nine states listed were "fully targeted," remaining on both parties' target list the entire campaign. Partially targeted are the fourteen states that appeared on one of the lists for at least part of the campaign. The other twenty-eight states (and DC) were never targeted by either party.

The lowest number is New Hampshire with ten visits. Nevada and Colorado, two states that could be considered partially targeted as they were on the list at one time or another (though not on both lists the entire time), each had eleven visits, one more than New Hampshire, while West Virginia, another partially targeted state, also had ten visits. There were five other partially targeted states[21] that received between four and eight visits, as did two non-targeted states.[22] No other state received more than two visits.[23]

Second, we can see this difference in the advertising of the campaigns.

Again, targeted states were inundated with ads; others were not. For example, the week of October 7–13 saw 12,802 ads in Florida, none in California.[24] Table 4-2 lists the number of ads by state during "prime campaign season" (the period between September 26 and the election).

TABLE 4-2: Number of Peak-Season Television Ads by State

		Ads	% US Ads			Ads	% US Ads
FL	T	55,477	22.25%	WA	P	1,763	0.71%
OH	T	44,131	17.70%	MO	P	1,687	0.68%
PA	T	30,228	12.12%	HI	P	1,307	0.52%
WI	T	24,152	9.69%	NC	N	703	0.28%
IA	T	17,935	7.19%	LA	P	682	0.27%
MI	T	13,328	5.35%	AR	P	615	0.25%
NM	T	12,141	4.87%	OK	N	575	0.23%
CO	P	9,751	3.91%	TN	P	541	0.22%
NV	P	8,252	3.31%	AL	N	254	0.10%
MN	T	6,108	2.45%	SC	N	96	0.04%
NH	T	5,929	2.38%	AZ	N	95	0.04%
WV	P	5,923	2.38%	DC	N	13	0.01%
ME	P	4,515	1.81%	NY	N	6	0.00%
OR	P	3,400	1.36%	TX	N	1	0.00%

Figures are the number of ads run in each state from September 26 until Election Day as compiled by FairVote and found in their report *Who Picks the President*, available at www.fairvote.org/presidential.
States not listed saw no ads during this time period.
T = Fully Targeted (on both parties' list the entire campaign); P = Partially Targeted (on the list of at least one of the parties for at least part of the campaign); N = Not Targeted by either party at any time during the campaign.

The top seven states, all fully targeted, saw 79 percent of the ads, and the nine fully targeted states saw a total of 84 percent of the ads. The fourteen partially targeted states saw 15.4 percent of the ads, while the other twenty-eight states (including DC) saw less than 1 percent of the ads (a total of 1,648 ads in those twenty-eight states, a number exceeded by seventeen individual states).[25] And these differences underestimate the contrast, as they do not account for advertising prior to September 26. Between March and September, for example, there were 14,273 campaign ads in Toledo, Ohio, none in California.[26] Thus, in terms of both visits by the candidates and television advertising, there were enormous differences between those states seen as in play and those seen as safely in the camp of one or the other of the campaigns.

TABLE 4-3: Peak-Season Campaign Index: States Above the Mean

Rank	State	Target	Index
1	Iowa	T	8.29
2	Ohio	T	4.66
3	New Hampshire	T	4.52
4	Wisconsin	T	4.46
5	New Mexico	T	4.22
6	Florida	T	4.05
7	Nevada	P	3.79
8	Pennsylvania	T	2.77
9	Minnesota	T	2.69
10	Colorado	P	2.04
11	Michigan	T	1.77
12	Maine	P	1.40
13	Oregon	P	1.09
14	West Virginia	P	1.03

Figures are the Peak-Season (Sept. 26 through Election Day) Campaign Index: (% of visits + % of ad $)/2/% of U.S. Population in given state. As compiled by FairVote and found in the report *Who Picks the President*, available at www.fairvote.org/presidential. Only those states above the mean of 1.0 are listed.
T = Fully Targeted (on both parties' list the entire campaign); P = Partially Targeted (on the list of at least one of the parties for at least part of the campaign).

The organization FairVote put together a "Peak Season Campaign Attention Index" that combined the percentage of television ads and percentage of visits to each state between September 26 and Election Day, taking into account the size of the state in terms of population. The mean score for the index was 1.0, a score exceeded by only fourteen states, including all nine fully targeted states (none of which ranked lower than eleventh) and five partially targeted states (with Nevada the highest ranking of these states, coming in seventh with an Attention Index of 3.79). Table 4-3 displays this index for the fourteen states with an index score above 1.0.[27]

Finally, this imbalance is also reflected, not surprisingly, in the likelihood of a citizen being contacted by a political party about the campaign. In targeted states, citizens were inundated with phone calls and people knocking on their doors as the ground war was in full swing. In other states, this was much less likely to happen.[28] Table 4-4 shows the difference in the likelihood of being contacted depending upon whether a citizen lived in a targeted, partially targeted, or non-targeted state.[29] Further, it is important to remember that this table certainly underestimates the differences, as one contact is scored in the same way as multiple contacts, and in targeted states, the contacts were constant.[30]

TABLE 4-4: Party Contact by State Level of Targeting

	Full Target	Partial Target	Not Targeted
Party Contact	65.2%	50.7%	34.4%
No Party Contact	34.8%	49.3%	65.6%

Data is from the American National Election Study and made available through the InterUniversity Consortium for Political and Social Research (ICPSR). Respondents were placed in three categories, by state in which they lived classified as Fully Targeted (on both parties' list the entire campaign), Partially Targeted (on the list of at least one of the parties for at least part of the campaign), or Not Targeted by either party at any time during the campaign, and whether or not the respondent said he or she had been contacted by either or both of the political parties.

Thus, some citizens see almost nothing of the campaign, with few visits, few mailings, phone, or personal contacts, and no television advertising except for some national cable television buys. They could, of course, watch the network newscasts, the Sunday morning talk shows, parts of the conventions, and the debates, and if they had cable or satellite television, they could watch quite a bit more coverage, but there is little effort to reach out and bring them into the campaign. And they know that their vote would not, in a sense, count at all. On the other hand, the citizens in the competitive states, especially in 2004 in Florida, Ohio, and Pennsylvania—the three states that, by the end of the campaign, were seen as the key to the election—were overwhelmed. And they, too, were dissatisfied with the campaign. In particular, the enormous advertising effort and the budgets that go with it lead to feelings of cynicism about the system.

Clearly, presidential candidates have always targeted their strategy to win state electoral votes, but the impact on election campaigns and citizens has increased dramatically over the past forty years. In the party-centered campaigns of the nineteenth and early twentieth centuries, it was the state and local party organizations, not the national campaign, that was the locus of action. And state and local parties often had strong incentives to organize and bring voters to the polls, even if they were in a state where the outcome of the presidential election was never in doubt. Perhaps the best way to illustrate the change is to compare the way that campaigning for the presidency and the strategies involved have been described over the years.

V.O. Key, in the second edition of his classic text *Politics, Parties and Pressure Groups*, published in 1950, describes the presidential campaign organization in this way:

> Campaign organization consists of two kinds of party machinery. The permanent party organization—that is, the national chairman, the national committee, state and county committees, precinct captains and committeemen, and other party functionaries—comes to life during the campaign and carries a major part of the burden. The regular party machinery, however, is supplemented by additional party organs, spawned in great numbers during the course of a campaign.[31]

Fourteen years later, in his fifth and final edition of the same text (1964), Key describes presidential campaigns very differently. Now "the presidential candidate must be his own manager." And "the integration of state and local party machinery into the national campaign presents special problems...[as] the extension of national leadership and direction to state and local organizations...requires both diplomacy and good fortune."[32] State and local parties have gone from part of the main team to a group that needs to be managed by the campaign.

And Steve Wayne's *The Road to the White House 2004*, after describing a national campaign organization run by the candidate with a campaign manager, political director, press secretary, research team, and others, notes that in recent campaigns "most have been centralized, with a few individuals making the key strategic and tactical decisions; a few have been decentralized. Some have worked through or in conjunction with national and state party organizations; others have disregarded these groups and created their own field organizations." He notes further that "until the 1970s, the Democrats had stronger state parties and a weaker national base. As a consequence, their presidential candidates tended to rely more heavily on state party organizations than did the Republicans. In recent years Democratic presidential campaigns have designated regional and state coordinators to oversee state party efforts on their behalf."[33]

Thus what we see over the last forty years is a movement away from state and local control over presidential campaigns to one where centralized, candidate-centered campaigns oversee a national effort where state and local organizations are simply one of many potential tools to be employed. And this means that more and more decisions about the campaign and the level of effort of the campaign are made with strictly national goals—and the Electoral College map—in mind. We will look more closely at other aspects of this shift from a strong, party-centered campaign with an emphasis on state and local party organizations to a candidate-centered national campaign in chapter 5. For now, what we need to know is that this shift has led to a greater emphasis on targeting resources toward those states that are seen as competitive.

The technology of polling and targeting appeals has grown as well. As late as the mid-1960s, when polling was still much more expensive than it is now, candidates needed to cast a wider net in deciding which states to target, and so candidate resources were spread more fully throughout the nation. Campaigns were also much more likely to run national advertising campaigns. When most of the audience was watching one of the networks, it still made sense to buy advertisements that ran across the nation, even if one was paying for people who lived in states that "did not matter," especially since it was not easy to measure the competitiveness of a state in a scientific way. But as the network audiences shrank with the growth of more alternatives such as cable television; as the ability to measure the competitiveness of a state grew more precise and less expensive; and as technology developed to allow candidates to send ads for broadcast to local stations all over the country, candidates shifted their resources from national efforts to more targeted state (and cable) campaigns. This shift is relatively recent. Prior to 1992, most television ad buys seemed to be national, with occasional additional local ads.[34] But in 1992, the Clinton campaign limited its national ad buys with a conscious decision to focus on local buys in eighteen states.[35] Still, led by Perot, who bought almost exclusively at the national level, $72 million was spent on network advertising.

By 1992, the ability to quickly spot and target what other candidates were doing and to respond also reached new heights, encouraging campaigns to focus their effort on the markets where it was most likely to matter, rather than a more expensive national advertising response. In fact, Clinton media advisor Frank Greer confessed that his staff was able to intercept Bush satellite transmission of ads to local stations and to tailor a response to those ads before they were even broadcast.[36] By 1996, the amount spent on network ad buys had shrunk to $34 million, and in 2000 basically all of the candidates' television advertising was spent in local markets targeting battleground states. National network television ads were not to be found.[37] The 2004 election continued this pattern, as the candidates and groups poured money into battleground states and markets.[38] The Bush campaign did spend $20 million on national cable television ad buys to target demographic, not geographic, groups.[39] But a viewer without cable who lived in a state not targeted for its electoral votes would not have seen any television ads for the presidential election (and even those with cable would only see a limited number if they happened to be watching the selected cable stations), while those in targeted states saw these ads all the time.[40] And the same thing has happened to mailings, phone calls, and door knockings.[41] The campaign has largely disappeared in non-competitive states and become overwhelming in states that are "in play." As a result of the intersection of the Electoral College and modern campaign technology, then, citizens see either too much or too little of the campaign to optimize their interest in what is happening.

Alternatives to the Electoral College

One way to fix this problem would be to change the Electoral College, and there have been suggestions for reforming it since its inception. But for reasons that will be clear shortly, change in this system is unlikely to take place. In chapter 6 we will look at reforms that might allow our system to more easily reach its democratic potential, but here I want to focus on the argument for making changes in the constitutionally mandated structure of the Electoral College and look at why, no matter how meritorious those arguments might be, no such change is likely to occur. If we want to do something about the impact of this too-much, too-little pattern, we will have to look elsewhere.

One proposal for reform is to do away with the actual electors and go to a system that automatically assigns the electoral votes based on the vote in the state. This would have the advantage of eliminating the faithless elector issue and moving to a system where the public is the ultimate arbiter, not a group of elite leaders chosen to pick the president. The Electoral College evolved informally in that direction in the early nineteenth century, and such a move would formalize that change. But it would obviously do little to solve the other problems that alienate people from the system and would provide no changed incentives for candidates, parties, or citizens.

More substantively, there are four other common proposals for reform: the District Plan, the Bonus Plan, the Proportional Plan, and Direct Election. Under the District Plan, electoral votes would be assigned as they are now in Maine and Nebraska, one per congressional district, with a two-vote bonus for whoever carries the state. This would have the advantage of opening up the campaign, as candidates would need to be in many more states, since there would likely be some competitive districts in most places even if those districts were sprinkled in among many very safe districts. Thus, for example, even if most of the districts in the Chicago area were either safe for the Democrats or, in the more suburban areas, the Republicans, there would likely be a couple of districts in the area that were closer and more competitive. That would force candidates to pay attention to a media market in an area that under current rules they could largely ignore, so we would see more advertising dollars spread out more fully. But direct mail and other on-the-ground organizing efforts could still be targeted quite narrowly to those districts that are competitive, and—given the sophisticated gerrymandering that we now engage in, which leaves most congressional districts safely in the hands of one party—most people would still find themselves in places where they "did not matter," and candidates would still have little incentive to mobilize citizens in most places. In fact, the number of places where mobilization efforts would be targeted might actually shrink, not grow. For example, in recent presidential elections, Iowa has been a competitive state for candidates. But if we went to a district system, two of the five districts, and potentially three, would be relatively safe. Thus, the competition would be over the two more competitive districts and the two-vote bonus. But that makes Iowa "worth less" than it is now, and the same would be true in other competitive states as well. A national media campaign would be encouraged, but not national or even statewide ground campaigns. And the "distortions" of the results when compared to the national popular vote would be stronger under this system than the current system. Richard Nixon would have won the 1960 election. The Carter-Ford election would have ended in an Electoral College tie, though the Democratic House would have almost certainly chosen Carter. And George W. Bush would still have beaten popular-vote-winner Al Gore.

TABLE 4-5: Presidential Election Outcomes Under Alternative Plans

Election	Electoral College	Direct Election	Prop. Plan*	District Plan	Bonus Plan
2004	**Bush**	**Bush**	**Bush**	**Bush**	**Bush**
2000	**Bush**	**Gore**	**No one**	**Bush**	**Gore**
1996	**Clinton**	**Clinton**	**No one**	**Clinton**	**Clinton**
1992	**Clinton**	**Clinton**	**No one**	**Clinton**	**Clinton**
1988	**Bush**	**Bush**	**Bush**	**Bush**	**Bush**
1976	**Carter**	**Carter**	**Unclear****	**No one**	**Carter**
1968	**Nixon**	**Nixon**	**No one**	**Nixon**	**Nixon**
1960	**Kennedy**	**Kennedy**	**No one**	**Nixon**	**Kennedy**

* The Proportional Plan is divided to the nearest tenth.

** This is unclear, because under this plan Carter receives 269.5 votes. If we round up or count anything above 269, he wins, but if not, no one wins. This is an updated version of a table constructed by Dudley, Robert, and Gitelson, Alan, *American Elections: The Rules Matter* (New York: Longman, 2002), 151. (The vote details for elections prior to 2004 can be found in their table.) Their table was adapted from Polsby, Nelson, and Wildavsky, Aaron, *Presidential Elections,* 10th ed. (New York: Chatham House, 2000), 251.

The simplest reform proposal would be to eliminate the Electoral College and go to a system of Direct Election of the president. After all, every other election to federal office uses a simple system where the votes are added up, and whoever gets the most votes wins.[42] Under such a plan, in the elections of the modern era since 1960, only the 2004 election would have had a different outcome.[43] Clearly, however, candidate strategy would have to be different. If a vote is a vote no matter where the voter lives, candidates and parties have strong incentive to organize and mobilize everywhere, even in those areas where they are sure to do well and sure to do badly. In fact, we might be more likely to find parties and candidates mobilizing voters in their strongholds, because those are places where volunteers and workers are easier to find. Getting out those extra votes in, for example, New York City for the Democrats or Texas for the Republicans, would now make sense and be easy to accomplish rather than be a "waste" of resources. And the same would be true for target advertising and mailings. A national campaign would be in order, and citizens everywhere would feel as if their votes counted.

On the other hand, the machinery of elections would still be at the state and local level. The ballot would not be the same everywhere. Even the candidates, aside from the two major-party candidates, would be different. The rules of voting would not be the same everywhere. And so the election would still be filtered through the fifty states. Furthermore, critics of Direct Election note that the cost of running a campaign would go up dramatically, and candidates would need to run expensive national media campaigns to reach voters everywhere. But that would necessarily leave fewer resources for the kind of "on-the-ground" mobilization that is most likely to involve citizens in the process. In fact, too many television ads tend to turn people off, as they do not find the kinds of appeals made in thirty-second spots to be particularly enticing, even if they do—at least to some extent—respond to those ads. One advantage of the current system is that by focusing resources it allows candidates to undertake effective mobilization efforts in a few limited areas. This may be of little help to the vast majority who live outside these targeted areas, but a national campaign might, in fact, take up so much time and money that there would be even fewer people on the receiving end of more personal and engaging mobilization efforts.[44]

As a result of these complicating factors, some propose a Proportional Plan as a kind of compromise. This system would keep the Electoral College in place but assign electoral votes in each state on a proportional basis. In this way, every state would matter, but some places would matter more than others, allowing some more strategic targeting than the direct system would allow. In fact, though, there are two fatal flaws in this approach. First, it would lead to a structure of campaigning similar to the Direct Election plan, meaning that a very expensive national media campaign would be the centerpiece of the process. And while it would be possible to better target a ground campaign to specific locals than the Direct Election plan, it does not seem likely to do so in a way that would allow for much, if any, improvement in the current situation, where most citizens feel as if their votes do not count. More important, this system would siphon off votes from the two major parties to minor-party candidates, making it much more likely that the Electoral College would not produce a majority, sending the election into the House of Representatives. In fact, no candidate would have won a majority in the Electoral College in 1960, 1968, 1992, 1996, or 2000, or possibly (depending upon how a majority was defined) 1976. And a system where the House of Representatives, not the public (even indirectly), is regularly choosing the president does not seem likely to create confidence in the system.

Finally, the problems with all of these options has led to a proposal known as the Bonus Plan, which would give 102 bonus electoral votes to the winner of the national popular vote. This plan would create incentives for a national campaign, as winning the national vote would almost certainly insure an Electoral College victory, since the likelihood of winning the national vote but losing the state-by-state electoral vote by more than 102 votes seems almost impossible. At the same time, the current Electoral College incentives to focus only on competitive states as opposed to every state would still, at least to some extent, remain in place, allowing for a more targeted, less expensive organizing and mobilizing strategy. And every citizen would feel as if his or her vote counted, even if some still seemed to count a bit more than others.

But in the end, making any change seems unlikely, no matter how strong the desire for change might be. There are two paths to change. One is to proceed on a state-by-state level. Using this approach, neither Direct Election nor the Bonus Plan is possible, but states are free to adopt the District Plan and could adopt some version of the Proportional Plan, providing it rounded off to whole numbers so that actual electors could be chosen.[45] But the likelihood of such changes is slim, because it is in the interests of the states to keep the winner-take-all system unless all states change. States that switch to such a system would diminish their influence. Instead of competing, for example, for twenty electoral votes in Ohio, the competition would be for five electoral votes.[46] An attempt by citizens in Colorado to use an initiative to change their system to a proportional one was defeated in 2004, as both major parties campaigned against it.

Thus, state-by-state efforts are unlikely to be successful except in relatively small states such as Maine and Nebraska, whose influence is unlikely to be very large no matter what system is used. The only method of reform that is likely to succeed, then, is a national change that would seem to require an amendment to the Constitution. But that seems as unlikely as waiting for the individual states to agree to dilute their own power by adopting the district or proportional schemes. The politics of passing a constitutional amendment on this topic require a dynamic that seems unlikely, if not impossible. First, there is the problem of agreeing upon a change. As noted above, there are a number of proposals, none of which is perfect. Each has strengths and weaknesses. From the perspective of citizen acceptance and support, the Direct Election plan might be the most attractive, but others would prefer the mix of incentives that flow from the alternative proposals that have been suggested. Finding a plan that two-thirds of both the House and Senate could support is unlikely, and even if that could be done, finding three-quarters of the states to agree to some plan that will certainly dilute the influence of some of those states seems impossible.

The only incentive for change would seem to be a public outcry and demand for change. Without an aroused and concerned public, the political incentives to keep the system will outweigh the philosophical desire to have a system that the public might find fairer, simpler, and more attractive. But this is not an issue that gains much public attention. It is very low in visibility, and people are unlikely to be concerned. The only time it is likely to rise higher in our public consciousness is when the winner of the popular vote loses in the Electoral College. But those are precisely the circumstances when change is unlikely, because that would require the president's supporters (or at least a good portion of them) to agree that their candidate "should have lost." No president seems likely to admit that we should have a system that "would have elected my opponent," as that will undermine the credibility and political strength of the president, and his or her partisan allies in Congress and in the states will have similar incentive to argue that the system that elected the president is a good one. The constitutional amendment process, with its supermajority requirements, is far too inhospitable to the political dynamic that such a battle is likely to entail. It is true that the public might express some concern after a "near miss" such as 1976, but "near misses" do not arouse the level of concern that an actual "wrong winner" creates. And the lack of movement for change after 2000, when the popular-vote winner was not elected president, is indicative of the limited prospects for change. Republicans were not going to argue that we needed a new system that would have "properly elected Al Gore and not George W. Bush." Democrats may have been angry and did try to use that anger to mobilize supporters in 2004, but it simply was not important enough to lead to any serious reform proposals.[47]

The problems with our presidential election system, then, are unlikely to be fixed by a major change in the Electoral College or other reforms requiring constitutional amendments. But there are other ways to improve both the nominating and finance systems and to rebuild the system in ways that regain democratic control of how our presidents are selected. Thus far, the primary focus of the discussion has been on how the system works and how that influences candidate behavior. Before looking at those potential reforms, we need to focus on the way citizens and political parties—the other crucial participants in the system—have responded to the changes that have occurred. As we will see, it is changes in these actors that are most likely to allow us to reclaim the election process.

Notes

1 See White, Theodore, *The Making of the President 1960* (New York: Pocket Books, 1961), especially ch. 10. Also, *A Study of Political Strategy and Tactics* (Washington, DC: The American Institute for Political Communication, 1967), ch. 4.

2 Nixon, Richard, *Six Crises* (Garden City, NY: Doubleday, 1962), 320.

3 For a fuller discussion of the history of the Electoral College, see Peirce, Neal, and Longley, Lawrence, *The People's President: The Electoral College in American History and the Direct Vote Alternative*, rev. ed. (New Haven, CT: Yale University Press, 1981); and Longley, Lawrence, and Peirce, Neal, *The Electoral College Primer 2000* (New Haven, CT: Yale University Press, 1999).

4 Roche, John, "The Founding Fathers: A Reform Caucus in Action," *American Political Science Review* 55 (1961): 811.

5 See Longley and Peirce, *The Electoral College Primer 2000*, 29.

6 See Dudley, Robert, and Gitelson, Alan, *American Elections: The Rules Matter* (New York: Longman, 2002), 133 and 156, n. 7.

7 For a look at these procedures and a table examining the method used by each state, see Berns, Walter, ed., *After the People Vote: A Guide to the Electoral College* (Washington, DC: American Enterprise Institute, 1992), 10–11 and appendix C. Also, Dudley and Gitelson, *American Elections*, 32–33.

8 For a description of all of the faithless electors and the circumstances surrounding their decisions, see the website of the Center for Voting and Democracy, www.fairvote.org/e_college/faithless.htm. Note that while presidential faithless electors have never had much impact, when twenty-three Virginia electors refused in 1836 to support the Democratic nominee for vice-president, Richard Johnson, because of allegations that he had lived with an African American, that left Johnson short of an electoral majority, forcing the selection into the U.S. Senate. The Senate did choose Johnson.

9 See Peirce and Longley, *The People's President*, 44–47.

10 Letter to George Hay, 23 August 1823, printed in Farrand, Max, ed., *The Records of the Federal Constitutional Convention of 1787*, vol. 3 (New Haven, CT: Yale University Press, 1937), 459.

11 For a good discussion of the struggle in the House over this decision, see Peirce and Longley, *The People's President*, 36–41.

12 As it turned out, that was crucial. Some Texas Democrats did go to court to argue that both Cheney and Bush were Texans and, thus, the Texas electors could not vote for both

of them. The U.S. District Court for the Northern District of Texas, in *Jones* v. *Bush*, 122F.Supp. 2d 713, however, ruled in Cheney's favor. Had the decision been upheld, Cheney would not have had a majority without the Texas electoral votes, and that would have sent the election to the Senate. The Senate, however, was evenly divided, 50-50, which would have given the tie-breaking vote to the vice-president at the time, Al Gore.

13 No change in the Florida vote could have changed the outcome of the popular-vote result. There are many books that discuss the 2000 election and the battle over Florida. Some of the more interesting are: The Correspondents of *The New York Times*, *36 Days: The Complete Chronicle of the 2000 Presidential Election Crisis* (New York: Times Books, 2001); Dionne, E.J., Jr., and Kristol, William, eds., *Bush* v. *Gore: The Court Cases and the Commentary* (Washington, DC: Brookings Institution Press, 2001); Kellner, Douglas, *Grand Theft 2000: Media Spectacle and a Stolen Election* (Lanham, MD: Rowman & Littlefield, 2001); Zelnick, Robert, *Winning Florida: How the Bush Team Fought the Battle* (Stanford, CA: Hoover Institution Press, 2001); Dershowitz, Alan, *Supreme Injustice: How the High Court Hijacked Election 2000* (New York: Oxford University Press, 2001); Posner, Richard, *Breaking the Deadlock: The 2000 Election, the Constitution and the Courts* (Princeton, NJ: Princeton University Press, 2001); Sabato, Larry, ed., *Overtime: The Election 2000 Thriller* (New York: Longman Publishers, 2002); and Tapper, Jake, *Down and Dirty: The Plot to Steal the Presidency* (New York: Little Brown, 2001).

14 The extremely corrupt election of 1876 lends itself to the possible interpretation that an honest count of the votes would have found Hayes the victor. But at the time of the election, both parties' tallies showed Tilden to be the popular-vote winner. See DiClerico and Ulsner, *Few Are Chosen*, 145, and Haworth, Paul, *The Hayes-Tilden Disputed Election of 1876* (New York: Russell and Russell, 1966).

15 In 1824, Andrew Jackson received more popular votes than John Quincy Adams, but there were still six states that did not use the popular vote, including New York. So the validity of the reported popular vote as a reflection of the national popular vote is unclear.

16 For a more extended explanation, see Longley and Peirce, *The Electoral College Primer 2000*, 48–51.

17 Some of this difference may be due to shifts in population and movement in and out of the states since the last census, rather than the turnout rate in the state, a problem that becomes more severe the further away from the census the election is held. But in either case, the point remains that electoral votes are not tied to how many people actually vote, which in effect penalizes people who live in high-turnout or fast-growing states.

18 Nagourney, Adam, "Candidates Face Sprawling and Complex Electoral Map," *The New York Times*, 12 May 2004, A18.

19 In two cases, Nevada and Colorado, Democratic hopes caused both parties to continue activities through the campaign, though not at the level of the other highly targeted states.

20 For a brief discussion of the targeting in the 2004 campaign, see Ceaser, James, and Busch, Andrew, *Red Over Blue* (Lanham, MD: Rowman & Littlefield, 2005), 132–35; and Pomper, Gerald, "The Presidential Election," in Nelson, Michael, *The Elections of 2004* (Washington, DC: CQ Press, 2005), 53–58.

21 Missouri (eight visits), Oregon (six), Arizona, Maine (both five), and New Jersey (four).

[22] New York and North Carolina (both five visits). The New York visits almost certainly involved fundraising. The North Carolina figure reflects the fact that it was the home state of Democratic vice-presidential candidate John Edwards.

[23] For a full list of visits by each of these candidates by state, see Pomper, "The Presidential Election," table 3-5, 55.

[24] See The World Watch Institute, "Matters of Scale—Advertising War for a War President," at www.worldwatch.org/node/802.

[25] See FairVote, *Who Picks the President*, a report by FairVote found at www.fairvote.org/presidential.

[26] See The World Watch Institute, "Matters of Scale."

[27] See FairVote, *Who Picks the President.*

[28] One clear exception to this rule was South Dakota, a state not seen as competitive at the presidential level but where enormous activity was undertaken in the Senate election where then-Majority Leader Tom Daschle was defeated by Republican challenger John Thune. See Theiss-Smith, Elizabeth, and Braunstein, Richard, "The Nationalization of Local Politics in South Dakota," in Magleby, David; Monson, Quin; and Patterson, Kelly, eds., *Dancing Without Partners* (Provo, UT: Brigham Young University, Center for the Study of Elections and Democracy, 2005), 232–48.

[29] The American National Election Study, from which this data is derived, was not drawn to produce random samples in every state, so actual statistical comparisons of the differences based on state are not possible. Many states, including one targeted state, New Mexico, had no respondents in the survey. This table is based on the unweighted numbers of respondents dividing people into the appropriate state category.

[30] For a discussion of the ground war in four targeted states (Ohio, Iowa, Florida, and New Mexico) and one partially targeted state (Missouri), see the case study chapters in Magleby et al., *Dancing Without Partners*.

[31] Key, V.O., *Politics, Parties and Pressure Groups*, 2nd ed. (New York: Thomas Y. Crowell, 1950), 20.

[32] Key, V.O., *Politics, Parties and Interest Groups*, 5th ed. (New York: Thomas Y. Crowell, 1965), 457–59.

[33] Wayne, Steven, *The Road to the White House 2004* (Belmont, CA: Thomson/Wadsworth, 2004), 197–98.

[34] Specific data prior to 1992 is hard to find because it was not compiled in any one place. Textbooks on presidential campaigns simply argued that decisions about where and how to make ad buys were contracted out by campaigns to advertising professionals, so that even campaigns did not have full information about this. The discussion focused on targeting demographic groups, not geographic groups, so the issues tended to be what shows to advertise on, not which markets. See, for example, Kessel, John, *Presidential Campaign Politics*, 2nd ed. (Homewood, IL: The Dorsey Press, 1984), 131. The pattern since 1992 is clear, and there is nothing about prior campaigns to indicate that the shift away from network ads since 1992 represents any kind of departure from previous trends in a different direction.

[35] See West, Darrell; Kern, Montague; Alger, Dean; and Goggin, Janice, "Ad Buys in Presidential Campaigns," *Political Communications* 12 (1995): 275–90; and West,

Darrell, *Air Wars*, 3rd ed. (Washington, DC: CQ Press, 2001), especially ch. 3.

36 Cited in West, *Air Wars*, 24. See also Kurtz, Howard, "In Advertising Give and Take, Clinton Took and Responded," *The Washington Post*, 6 November 1992, A10.

37 West, *Air Wars*, 39.

38 For example, in the battleground state of Iowa, in the Des Moines television market, the Kerry and Bush campaigns spent $5.2 million on television ad buys, and when parties and outside groups are added in, the total is over $9 million. See Sanders, Arthur, "Taking It to the Streets: The Iowa Presidential Campaign of 2004," in Magleby et al., *Dancing Without Partners*, ch. 4.

39 Seelye, Katharine, "How to Sell a Candidate to a Porsche-Driving, Leno-Loving Nascar Fan," *The New York Times*, 6 December 2004, A16.

40 To cite Des Moines again—Kerry and Bush ran a total of almost 10,000 ads in that market, and adding in parties and outside groups brought the total to over 16,600. See Sanders, "Taking It to the Streets."

41 See Magleby et al., *Dancing Without Partners*, for case studies of activities in five states including four that were heavily targeted: Florida, New Mexico, Iowa, and Ohio.

42 For a discussion of various reform proposals, see Schumaker, Paul, and Loomis, Burdett, eds., *Choosing a President: The Electoral College and Beyond* (Chatham, NJ: Chatham House, 2002). For a defense of the Electoral College, see Gregg, Gary, ed., *Securing Democracy: Why We Have an Electoral College* (Boulder, CO: Westview, 2001).

43 This, of course, assumes the votes as cast in these elections using the Electoral College system. Had we actually used a different system, candidate strategy would have been different, and this result might not have been different. That is, if Bush and Gore operated under different rules, the outcome might have been the same.

44 Still, there are many who argue that these costs do not outweigh the advantages that such a system would have. However, as we will see shortly, the likelihood of actually making such a change is quite small at best.

45 The Supreme Court upheld the right of states to use the district system in *McPherson* v. *Blacker* (1892), and the language of that case makes it likely that the courts would uphold the right of states to choose electors on a proportional basis. However, those proportions would need to lead to whole people being chosen, unlike the version that rounds to tenths in table 4-5. To use the more proportionally accurate version in the table would require a constitutional amendment, as it would require eliminating actual electors.

46 In 2000, there were only three congressional districts in Ohio where Gore and Bush were separated by less than 5 percent of the vote. Using that as a guide going into 2004 would have led to those three districts plus the bonus of two for the state as "in play." Using a more expansive definition of competitive, that is, decided by less than 10 percent in 2000, would have added another four districts to the list.

47 In addition, the fiasco in Florida led to a push for other kinds of electoral reform involving ballot access and clarity, which occupied the efforts of those who desired electoral reform and also drew attention away from the fact that Al Gore had won the national popular vote. This diluted the potential pressure for change by channeling public attention and Democratic efforts at a different level of reform. But it seems doubtful that even had the problems in Florida not dominated the attention of those interested in the electoral proc-

ess, a push for a constitutional amendment premised on the idea that "the wrong person won" could have gained much momentum.

CHAPTER 5

Declining Involvement: Voters and Parties and Presidential Elections

Presidential elections, as we have seen, have been shaped by the rules of nomination, election, and finance in ways that have pushed candidates to behave in a manner that weakens the democratic foundations of our electoral system. But before we can look more closely at how we might rebuild that system, we need to take a closer look at the impact of these systemic factors on the other main actors in our system: citizens/voters and the organizations that work to organize and involve those citizens—primarily the two parties, but also interest groups. It should be clear from previous discussion that these changes have been alienating to citizens, turning them off to the possibilities of democratic politics. And the roles of political parties and interest groups have been transformed in ways that encourage this trend, though, as we shall see, some developments in technology provide opportunities for political parties to once again transform themselves, this time in more democratically efficacious ways. But such a transformation will not be easy, as the decline in citizen attachment to the process has been long and deep and will not easily be reversed. To understand why that is so, we need to look more closely at that decline.

The Decline in Voter Turnout

Beginning in 1960, a slow and steady decline in voter turnout began. As seen in table 5-1, with the exception of a small upturn in 1992, that decline was steady until 2000, when a forty-year trend reversed itself for two consecutive elections, with turnout rising in 2004 to levels not seen since 1972. The decline in turnout has been the subject of numerous books and articles and some debate.[1] Let us begin by examining the decline and the various theories that purport to explain that decline before we examine the arguments that claim that the decline is not as large as the numbers in table 5-1 seem to indicate.

As Rosenstone and Hansen note, picking up an argument first made by Richard Brody in 1978,[2] this decline in turnout is troubling because of what we know about the factors that lead to higher voter turnout. In particular, the single demographic factor that is most strongly related to higher political participation is education. The evidence is very clear. The higher the level of education, the more likely people are to vote.

TABLE 5.1: Voter Turnout in Presidential Elections, 1952–2004			
Year	Turnout	Year	Turnout
1952	61.6	1980	52.8
1956	59.3	1984	53.3 (continued)
1960	62.8	1988	50.3
1964	61.4	1992	55.3
1968	60.7	1996	49.0
1972	55.1	2000	50.3
1976	53.6	2004	55.5
Figures are the percentage of the voting-age population casting votes for president of the United States as determined by the U.S. Census Bureau. The data is found in table 407 of the *Statistical Abstract of the United States: 2006*, found at www.census.gov/prol/www/statistical-abstract.html.			

According to the American National Election Study, for example, in 2004, 93 percent of those with at least a college degree voted, while only 51 percent of those without a high school degree went to the polls.[3] This relationship between education and political participation is very robust. It has been found everywhere. And according to the most comprehensive study of voting behavior done in the past forty years, using census files, education is the single most important determinant of voting.[4] What makes this a confounding fact is that since 1960, the level of education of the American public has been on a steady increase. As can be seen in table 5-2, the percentage of the population with four or more years of college has been increasing, though that increase has recently slowed. So we would expect a steady increase in voter turnout. That has not happened.

Similarly, we know that the rules that govern ballot access have a strong impact on voter turnout.[5] And the United States, with its various state regulations regarding voting and registration, has more complicated and restrictive rules than most industrial democracies. The most careful analysis of the impact of restrictive rules on turnout estimates that easing such restrictions would increase voter turnout by between 8 and 15 percent.[6] But again, in terms of these trends, the time period in which this decline in voter turnout occurred did witness major changes that eased restrictive voting practices. The most important of these changes was the passage of the Voting Rights Act in 1965, which led to the enfranchisement of millions of African Americans who had not been able to vote previously. To take the starkest example, the percentage of African Americans registered to vote in Mississippi went from 6.7 percent in 1964 to 59.5 percent in 1968. No other state witnessed growth of that magnitude, but every state in the old Confederacy saw an increase of at least 12 percent, except for North Carolina (8.5 percent increase), Tennessee (2.4 percent increase), and Florida (a 1.7 percent decrease!), three states where the major jump took place earlier.[7] And according to Rosenstone and Hansen, voter turnout among African Americans jumped 35 percent in the fifteen years surrounding the passage of this and other pieces of civil rights legislation from the late 1950s through 1972, with almost half of that increase due directly to the impact of easing voter registration laws.[8]

TABLE 5-2: Levels of Education, General Public, 1950–2004

Year	Less than 5 years of Elementary School	High School or More (1)	4 years of College or More (2)
1950	11.1%	34.3%	6.2%
1960	8.3%	41.1%	7.7%
1970	5.3%	55.2%	11.0%
1980	3.4%	68.6%	17.0%
1990	2.5%	77.6%	21.3%
2000	1.6%	84.1%	25.6%
2004	1.5%	85.2%	27.7%

(1) Figures prior to 2000 are for all persons with at least four years of high school.

(2) Figures for 2000 and 2004 are for persons with a bachelor's degree or higher.

Data comes from the U.S. Census Bureau and was compiled by Information Please Database, Pearson Education, Inc. It is available at www.infoplease.com/ipa/A0779809.html.

Other efforts were also made in this period to increase the level of voter turnout. The Supreme Court ruled in 1970 that the passage of the Voting Rights Act Amendments of 1970, which, among other things, restricted the ability of states to impose residency restrictions on voters, was constitutional and the Court has made it clear that, basically, voter registration rolls cannot be closed earlier than thirty days prior to the election.[9] States can impose restrictions of up to fifty days on non-presidential elections,[10] but almost all citizens can now register to vote for all elections in the month prior to Election Day. Minnesota, Maine, and Wisconsin have allowed Election Day registration since the 1970s, with New Hampshire, Idaho, and Wyoming moving to Election Day registration and North Dakota eliminating voter registration entirely in the early 1990s. According to Rosenstone and Hansen, same-day registration leads to an average increase in turnout of 3 percent over states with thirty-day residency requirements.[11] But other studies find a stronger impact. The most widely cited and careful study, by Craig Brians and Bernard Grofman, estimates that allowing Election Day registration in all states would boost turnout by 7 percent.[12] A study by Stephen Ansolabehere and David Konisky, using panel data as opposed to cross-sectional data, argues that the impact found in previous studies may overestimate the effect of Election Day registration,[13] and Rosenstone and Hansen could find no evidence that the easing of residency requirements had resulted in an appreciable increase in voter turnout over time.[14] But the weight of the evidence does seem to indicate that easing registration requirements does lead to some increase in voter turnout, and the trend over the past forty years has been to ease those restrictions.[15]

There has also been a general trend toward making it easier for citizens to vote by what used to be called "absentee ballots" but is now simply referred to as "early voting." States that make such voting practices available have higher turnout than those that do not.[16] The number of citizens taking advantage of such opportunities has continued to grow to close to one-fifth of the electorate as of 2004. And Oregon has done away with polling places entirely, going to all-mail ballots, leading to some of the highest voter turnout levels in the nation.[17] While it may be true that these changes do not lead to increases as large as those suggested by their strongest supporters, it does seem clear that such changes should lead to at least some increase in voter turnout.[18]

Finally, we should mention the largest attempt to increase voter participation since the Voting Rights Act, the National Voter Registration Act (NVRA) of 1993, often referred to as the "Motor Voter Act." This law required that states make voter registration forms available at the time residents applied for or renewed their driver's licenses, that such opportunities also be made available at a number of other service agencies, and that states accept mail-in voter registration applications.[19] There was much controversy over this law, and many states initially refused to implement it. (There are still differences among the states in how they continue to implement it.) Conway's examination of the law's impact finds that it certainly does increase registration and that states that made the most significant changes in their procedures as a result of this law and those that implemented it most aggressively saw the largest increase in registration. But the impact on turnout was negligible. Still, it does provide a larger pool of voters, leading Conway to conclude that "NVRA can contribute to increased voter turnout when issues or candidates stimulate political involvement or when candidates conduct effective voter turnout drives to mobilize a targeted subset of those who have registered."[20]

The larger point to remember, then, is that this decline in turnout is occurring in an environment where demographic changes in educational levels and specific political changes designed to increase turnout are occurring. And this means that the trend of declining turnout is underestimating the impact of the factors that are at work. Before we look more closely at those factors, though, we need to look briefly at the strong challenge that has been made to this argument, by Michael McDonald and Samuel Popkin, that voter turnout is declining.[21]

McDonald and Popkin argue that while voter turnout did decline from 1960 through 1972, there has been no clear pattern since then. Turnout from 1972 through 2000 fell only slightly, and the appearance of declining turnout was an illusion. This illusion, they argue, stems from the fact that census figures used to determine the number of eligible voters fail to take into account that portion of the population that is not eligible to vote, particularly noncitizens, prison inmates, and convicted felons. Eliminating these people from the number of eligible voters, McDonald and Popkin argue, wipes away most of the decline since 1972.[22] But as Thomas Patterson argues, this decline in turnout is not an illusion.[23] First, he notes that in the South, African Americans and poor whites were often ineligible to vote, so during much of this period turnout in the South was actually rising by any measure, as these citizens were finally able to exercise the franchise. But if we look at the non-South, we see a much steeper decline, one that remains even when we look at estimates based on eligible voters as McDonald and Popkin urge, or the voting age population as the census figures do.[24]

Second, turnout in presidential primaries has also been dropping from nearly 30 percent in 1972 and 1976 to only 17 percent in 2000 and 13 percent in 1996 when only the Republicans held contested primaries.[25]

Third, turnout in non-presidential elections is also quite low. Patterson cites a study by Jack Doppelt and Ellen Shearer that found no examples of state and local elections where turnout had increased significantly but many where it had fallen, and concluded that turnout had become "an embarrassment."[26]

Fourth, as Pippa Norris argues, the decision not to allow noncitizens or convicted felons to vote is a political decision.[27] Other nations do allow these people to vote. And by preventing convicted felons from voting in most states, we disenfranchise approximately 13 percent of African American males, or 1.4 million people. In fact, it was estimated that in 2000, 4.7 million Americans lost their voting rights. Only two states, Maine and Vermont, and the District of Columbia allow inmates to vote. Thirty-six states still prohibit those on parole after being released from voting. Three states, Florida, Kentucky, and Virginia, permanently bar all convicted felons from voting, while nine others bar certain categories of convicted felons for life. And the process of restoring voting rights is, in most places, complicated.[28]

Finally, as we will see shortly, there are other measures that indicate a declining interest in and attachment to our presidential election system. Thus, while McDonald and Popkin are correct in highlighting the complexity of the issue of voter turnout and reminding us that most of the decrease in turnout since 1960 did occur in the 1960s, with the period since 1972 seeing much smaller decreases, the paradox of declining turnout remains. Our electorate has become more educated, and the rules governing voting have become more permissive. (An exception is laws concerning felons and noncitizens which, even if not more restrictive—though in some states they have become more restrictive—have affected more people.) But citizens have not responded. We do not vote, and that makes it more difficult for "the people" to exercise democratic control.

The Declining Attachment to Politics: Evidence Beyond Voter Turnout

The strongest arguments concerning the decline in civic engagement by the American public come from Robert Putnam. He makes the case that we have seen a steady disappearance of social capital and civic engagement since the 1960s.[29] Putnam focuses on a loss of social capital, which is defined as "the features of social life—networks, norms, and trust—that enable participants to act together more effectively."[30] According to Putnam, part of this loss can be seen in declining membership in many traditional local civic organizations. Putnam finds declining membership in organizations ranging from fraternal groups such as the Elks, to local civic groups such as the PTA, to social clubs such as bowling leagues. Participation, according to Putnam, has thus become more privatized. We send in a check rather than become involved face to face in ongoing social/civic structures. And this, he argues, weakens the ties of civic culture and life. We are less connected to the political system.

Similarly, examining a wide range of data—some of it the same as Putnam, some of it different—Rosenstone and Hansen document a decline of citizen involvement in organizations, clubs, and political parties. And this, they show, "weakens an important link in the process by which citizens are moved to participate in government. Participation in governmental politics declines as participation in associational activity declines."[31]

Putnam did find an upturn in some of his measures of social capital after the attacks of September 11, 2001, finding a small increase in episodic volunteering (about 6 percent) and in attendance at church or political meetings (under 5 percent), but no change in organizational membership.[32] But the opportunity to draw people into greater connection with civic life that might have resulted from 9/11 disappeared as the president used the event to call on Americans to resume their private lives and spend money to stimulate the economy.[33]

Putnam and others who focus on this decline in social capital are not without critics. These critics argue that Putnam focuses on "old forms" of civic engagement and that he misses participation in newer organizations such as issue-oriented groups.[34] And there has been an explosion in the number of advocacy groups present in American society, although these groups are different. They rely much more heavily on top-down activities, with professional management and "members"—if there are any members—whose assistance comes largely through checkbook contributions. Theda Skocpol's careful study of changes in American civic life summarizes these changes quite well:

> From the 1800s through the 1950s and 1960s, U.S. civic life was dominated by a mixture of business associations plus many kinds of representatively governed membership associations. Since the 1960s, however, the ranks of professionally run groups have swelled, especially groups other than business associations. Groups dispersing contributions from the wealthy; professionally run citizens' associations; and professionally managed advocacy groups for the poor and vulnerable—all of these types have expanded their presence on the U.S. civic scene. At the same time,

> representatively governed voluntary federations have ceased to proliferate, and their dues-paying memberships have contracted.
>
> A new civic America has thus taken shape since the 1960s, as professionally managed advocacy groups and institutions have moved to the fore, while representatively governed, nation-spanning voluntary membership federations—especially those with popular or cross-class memberships—have lost clout in national public affairs and faded from the everyday lives of most Americans."[35]

Thus, we have witnessed a decline in the involvement of Americans in civic life. Putnam's data and analysis may overstate that decline by focusing attention on more traditional styles of involvement and ignoring the changing nature of political activity, but even taking that change into account, it is clear that we have, over the last forty years, become less involved in the democratic process. Even Russell Dalton, one of the strongest proponents of the view that citizen politics has not declined but evolved, notes that Putnam has "identified important changes in the American political process." And Dalton argues that while "Americans are less likely to participate in institutionalized forms of social or political action, there is some evidence that engagement in informal groups, social movements and local initiatives are filling part of this void."[36] But his evidence seems to indicate that the declines found by Putnam do not seem to have been mirrored in other advanced industrialized democracies and that, in fact, citizen involvement in Europe has been on the rise, while the United States, even accounting for the changes in types of activity that Dalton is concerned with, has seen a decline in the connections that citizens have with the political system.

To sum up this set of trends, John Mark Hansen argues that it reflects a detachment of participation from place. We are less likely to be involved in politics through locally active, face-to-face kinds of groups. Instead, we become attached—to the extent that we do—through newsletters from groups soliciting our contributions. And this, he argues, "threatens citizen involvement in politics by separating activity from the social connections that encourage participation and from the social networks through which elites mobilize participation…. [P]olitical participation detached from place is tied part and parcel with the detachment of Americans from political involvement."[37] We vote less and we are less involved in social and political life.

And we can find other trends that fit this pattern. Our interest in political campaigns has been declining. As can be seen in table 5-3, the percentage of people very much interested in the campaign dropped from levels in the high 30s during the 1960s and early 1970s (with a lower drop in 1972) to levels in the high 20s to 30 in the 1980s, and then, after a jump to higher levels in 1992, to the lower 20s in 1996 and 2000. As with some other indicators, 2004 did show increased engagement, which we will look at more closely in chapter 6, but again, the pattern is one of less interest over time. And the figures for a general interest in public affairs, not simply the campaign (also in table 5-3), display a similar pattern.

TABLE 5-3: Interest in the Campaign and Public Affairs, 1960–2004

Year	Very Much Interested (1)	Most of the Time (2)
1960	38%	21%
1964	38%	30%
1968	39%	33%
1972	31%	36%
1976	37%	38%
1980	30%	26%
1984	28%	26%
1988	29%	22%
1992	39%	26%
1996	25%	21%
2000	26%	20%
2004	40%	26%

(1) Interest in the current campaign – very much, somewhat or not much.
(2) General interest in public affairs—most of the time, some of the time, only now and then, or hardly at all, except in 1960, when the choice was very closely, fairly closely, or not much at all.
Data comes from the American National Election Study Guide to Public Opinion and Electoral Behavior, available at:
(1) www.umich.edu/~nes/nesguide/toptable/tab6d_6.htm
(2) www.umich.edu/~nes/nesguide/toptable/tab6d_5.htm

Similarly, Thomas Patterson notes the declining attention paid to election news both on television and in newspapers and the declining audiences for televised presidential debates (which, it should be noted, still maintain audience numbers in the tens of millions). For each of the Kennedy-Nixon debates, approximately 60 percent of households with televisions watched. By 1984, that figure was down to 46 percent, declining further in 1988 to 36 percent. After the rebound seen in all of these trends in 1992, they dropped again to an average of 29 percent in 1996, and—in spite of a much closer election and a jump in the audience for the first debate from 36 million in 1996 to 47 million in 2000[38]—remained at that level in 2000, with the third Gore-Bush debate scoring an all-time low rating of 26 percent.[39] Audiences were up for the debates in 2004 to numbers matching those in 1992, with an estimated viewing audience of 63 million for the first debate and 46 million for the second debate;[40] but again, the clear trend is declining involvement.

TABLE 5-4: Various Measures of Trust in Government, 1964–2004

Election Year	64	68	72	76	80	84	88	92	96	00	04
(1) Trust Govt.	76	61	53	33	25	44	40	29	33	44	47
(2) Run for All	64	51	38	24	21	39	31	20	27	35	40
(3) Have Say	70	58	59	56	59	68	50	57	38	50	45
(4) Listens	32	23	17	11	8	15	13	12	15	16	16
(5) Officials Care	62	55	49	44	43	57	37	37	24	33	34
(6) Cause Attn.	65	60	55	52	51	42	37	47	42	44	56

(1) You can trust the federal government just about all of the time or most of the time.
(2) Government is run for the benefit of all.
(3) Disagree: "People like me don't have any say about what the government does."
(4) Government listens to the people a good deal of the time.
(5) Disagree: "Public officials don't care much what people like me think."
(6) Elections make the government pay a good deal of attention to what the public thinks.
All of these measures come from the American National Election Study Guide to Public Opinion and Political Behavior in section 5, "Support for the Political System." The index to locate all of the questions and responses is found at www.umich.edu/~nes/nesguide/gd-index.htm#6.

Finally, we can see the declining attachment to the political process in the public's dwindling trust in government and increasing sense that government does not pay attention to it. The patterns of responses to a series of questions asked in the American National Election Studies from 1964 through the present show the familiar pattern of basically declining trust in government from the 1960s through the present, with an occasional upturn, usually followed by more decline. Table 5-4 shows these patterns.

Whether the question is do we trust the government to do what is right; is the government run for the benefit of all or a few special interests; do people have a say in government; or how much does the government care or listen to the people, the patterns are the same. We feel more removed from government than we did in the past.[41] Perhaps most revealing, when it comes to these trends, are responses to the question of whether elections cause government to pay attention to the public. Here, too, we see a decline. Looking at the evidence of the relationship between trust and voter turnout, Conway concludes that while the evidence of a direct link between declining trust and declining turnout is unclear, "citizens who perceive one candidate as more trustworthy and more competent than another are more likely to vote in the election."[42] Thus, along with declining levels of trust, there is likely to be an electorate less likely to find such a candidate. All of these patterns, then, point in the same direction: an electorate that feels less connected to our political and electoral process and less engaged in democratic politics. The election of 2004 does offer some hope that these patterns may be changing, but before we examine that election more closely, we need to look at the role of political parties and other organizations as intermediaries between the public and our political institutions. Parties have been the traditional mechanism for mobilizing democratic activity and bringing people into the system, and the changing face of party involvement in presidential elections is central to understanding why citizens have been losing control of the process and how they might get that control back.

Political Parties in the Electoral Process

The declining role of political parties has been a staple of political science literature on elections and politics since the 1970s.[43] The changing nature of campaigning led to a decreasing role for parties in the electoral process. Parties used to supply the workers who were central to campaign communications. But as the system has evolved to one dependent on mass communication techniques to reach voters—particularly television—parties have been replaced by PACs, political consultants, and other campaign professionals. Money and professional expertise (in media, polling, marketing, etc.) replaced political experience and time as the coin of the campaign realm. And that led to a loss of control of campaigns by parties. Individual candidates could still rely on parties and the expertise and resources they could provide, but they were less dependent upon them, and campaigns became candidate-centered, not party-centered. The declining role of the national political party conventions as places for party debate and

tional political party conventions as places for party debate and decision was emblematic of this shift.

Still, we should not overestimate the decline of parties, and to the extent that parties were in decline in the 1970s and 1980s, that decline has been reversed. They are still central to our politics, in some ways as central as ever. As John Bibby notes, "In the post-1960s era, party organizations in the United States have changed from being loose confederations of state and local associations that mobilized local electorates, into national entities that direct resources, recruit candidates, and supply expertise."[44] Parties, then, reacted to this new environment by adapting. And in many ways the national parties became more important than they ever had been as they became more professional, providing the services that candidates needed.[45] Parties now

> serve their candidates by mobilizing and channeling the resources needed for successful campaigns. They are instrumental organizations geared to winning general elections for party standard-bearers whom they had only a modest role, if any, in selecting. Thus, by the traditional criteria of party strength [measured in terms of the voter-mobilizing activities of patronage and membership-based parties], today's national and state party organizations appear weak. [But] by other standards—professionalism, bureaucratization, resource development, and internal integration—the national and state organizations show renewed strength.[46]

However, in spite of their continuing relevance and strength as they adapted to this new role, at least through 2000, parties continued to lose much of their ability to draw citizens into the electoral process. In the pre-1960, more party-centered era, local parties were much more central, drawing people into the process and creating attachments with citizens that gave people a stake in the system. In the candidate-centered politics that developed and grew as we moved through the 1970s toward 2000, that role was largely lost. Instead, parties became facilitating organizations, linking the presidential candidates to other groups of supporters. This process was one that often left many citizens feeling ignored and alienated from the system and contributed to the declining attachment we have been examining. Ironically, as the parties "regained" strength, they did so in ways that did not reignite broad citizen attachment either to the parties or to the electoral system.

There are three aspects of this change in the relationship between parties and citizens in the presidential election process. First is the party's role in fundraising and supplying money to the campaign. The Federal Election

Campaign Act (FECA) of 1971, as amended in 1974, sharply constricted the role of political parties in the finance of presidential campaigns. The parties were treated much like any other group, that is, allowed to contribute $5,000 to the presidential campaign. But the party could engage in unlimited spending on "non-campaign activities" such as voter mobilization and education or issue advocacy,[47] an aspect of the law they would learn to exploit. And the law was soon amended to allow unlimited spending with funds that were raised as what was called "soft money." In 1976, the parties played a relatively limited role in the campaign, as the rules seemed to prohibit them from engaging in many "typical" party activities, such as handing out buttons or lawn signs. Partly in response to this, and partly to clarify some other aspects of the law that were felt to need fixing, amendments to the law were added in 1979 that allowed the national parties to funnel money to state and local parties, even if the state and local parties were using the money for the express purpose of influencing federal elections.

As it became clear that the issue-advocacy aspect of the law would allow financing ads that mentioned candidates by name as long as they did not "expressly advocate" their election or defeat,[48] the parties became much bolder in the use of such ads. By 1996, the parties were not only giving large amounts of soft money to state and local parties; they were actually telling the state parties which advertisements to buy with the money and when and where to air those ads. The FEC staff tried to challenge these practices, recommending in 1998 that both the Clinton and Dole campaigns repay millions of dollars to the federal treasury, because these party issue ads "violated the spending limits of the Federal election laws and should have counted as contributions to the presidential campaigns."[49] But two weeks later the FEC commissioners unanimously rejected that recommendation, allowing the parties complete freedom to coordinate federal campaigns without limits through the state parties and their own purchase of issue ads. Thus, by 2000, one way the parties had "come back" was by reasserting themselves as the center for campaign finance. The skyrocketing amount of money spent by the parties can be seen in table 5-5. Money flowed through the parties' soft-money accounts to state and local parties, and these parties were instructed as to how to spend that money. In addition, the parties' own hard-money accounts could also finance large amounts of "independent spending." The parties were not, as they had been, groups of volunteers and neighbors who knocked on doors and drew people into politics in a personal way (though this aspect of parties did still exist). They were large institutions in Washington that were fueling public sentiment that too much money was being spent on political campaigns.

TABLE 5-5: Party Spending, 1992–2004				
	1992	1996	2000	2004
Democrats, Hard Money	$239.1	$253.7	$296.7	$683.6
Democrats, Soft Money	$48.9	$147.6	$267.3	0
Democrats Total	**$288.0**	**$401.3**	**$564.0**	**$683.6**
Republicans, Hard Money	$359.9	$491.6	$491.8	$755.3
Republicans, Soft Money	$67.1	$170.3	$268.7	0
Republicans Total	**$427.0**	**$661.9**	**$760.5**	**$755.3**
Overall Party Total	**$815.0**	**$1,063.2**	**$1,324.5**	**$1,438.9**

Figures are in millions of dollars adjusted for inflation (2004 dollars). Figures are from the Federal Election Commission. The data for 1996, 2000, and 2004 are compiled and adjusted for inflation in Magleby, David; Monson, J. Quin; and Patterson, Kelly, eds., *Dancing Without Partners* (Provo, UT: Brigham Young University, Center for the Study of Elections and Democracy, 2005), table 1-4, p. 45. The data for 1992 are in FEC press release, "FEC Reports Increase in Party Fundraising in 2000," May 15, 2001, with the adjustment for inflation done at the Department of Labor, Bureau of Labor Statistics inflation calculator found at http://data.bls.gov/cgi-bin/cpicalc.pl.

We should be clear. This shift in roles did not cause the decline of party-centered campaigns. That trend had begun much earlier and was, by this time, complete. Rather, the shift reflected an adaptation of the parties to the new environment in which they found themselves. But that adaptation reinforced and exacerbated the sense of disconnect that citizens were feeling about parties and campaigns. As we have already briefly noted in chapter 3 and will examine more fully in chapter 6, the changes in the laws of campaign finance enacted after the 2000 election and the subsequent adaptation of the parties to that change have led to some practices that may reconnect citizens to parties and the campaign process, but there are other aspects of that law that may work against these more positive trends. For now, we simply need to note that this shift in party function to financier did little to encourage positive public attitudes about campaigns, even if it did prove that those predicting the end of parties were completely off-base.

The second way in which party-candidate relations have changed involves the use of political consultants. As Paul Herrnson notes, "Although it was initially believed that the rise of political consultants and the proliferation of PACs would hasten the decline of political parties, recent evidence suggests that political consultants and PACs are seeking to cooperate with the political parties rather than destroy them."[50]

As campaigns became candidate-centered, the concern was that consultants would replace political parties, as candidates could now get the services they needed to run campaigns—services formerly supplied by parties—from political consultants.[51] But again, the parties were able to adapt and not be replaced. Parties found that consultants could provide help for candidates in certain areas, particularly those related to communication/message and those that are technical in nature. At the same time, parties retained a larger role in areas that require large staffs and that are time-, not money-intensive, such as opposition research and get-out-the-vote drives.[52] Further, as Robin Kolodny has found, most political consultants are allied with—not adversaries to—parties. Her 1997 survey of consultants found that 88.6 percent of consultants were allied with one party rather than working for candidates allied with both or neither party. Also, a majority of consultants indicated that they had parties as clients and that they regularly consulted with the parties during the normal course of their work. Finally, a survey she did of all of the state parties' executive directors found that almost all of them (38 of the 40 who replied) said that they recommend consultants to candidates, indicating that we have developed a consulting system where these independent contractors work in partisan circles. They complement the work of parties, and candidates come to rely on the parties for advice as to who might be a good consultant; even if they do not, the consultants regularly reach out to and maintain contact with the parties.[53] Thus, we have developed a system where, in the words of Dulio and Nelson, "Consultants and parties are currently engaged in an electoral partnership in which there is a clear division of labor between the two actors. Services are divided between those centered on message creation and delivery and those that require a great deal of staff resources and time, with consultants being the main service provider of the former and parties of the latter."[54]

But as Kolodny further notes, this cooperative notion relies on a particular aspect of political parties, their organizational infrastructure. Here there is clearly cooperation. But when we consider the party in the electorate—that is, the connection that citizens feel toward the parties—this cooperative, symbiotic relationship is not as evident. Here we find consultants working to undermine the connections citizens feel with parties. The role of the consultant is to help the candidate craft a message that will get her or him elected. In that capacity, consultants "encourage voters to come up with conclusions about candidates on their own, abandoning whatever party feeling they may have if that would help the consultant's client."[55] Again, while parties have adapted and learned how to co-exist with outside consultants, they have done so in a way that discourages citizens from feeling connected to the parties and, through them, to the broader political system.

Finally, the third aspect of the changing nature of parties that has led to continuing citizen disillusionment is the relationship between parties and the interest groups that support them. The parties of the past often relied on traditional patronage to connect with their supporters. But that basis of party support has been in decline for an extended period of time as a result of civil service laws and a growth in the strength and role of public employee unions. And Supreme Court decisions, particularly *Eldred* v. *Burns* in 1976, in which the Court ruled that the Cook County (Chicago) Democrats could no longer fire people on the basis of their party affiliation, have confirmed and strengthened this trend.[56] This shift has led to a well-documented change, with parties relying on "amateurs"—volunteers who are committed to the party for ideological reasons—to make up the core of their organization.[57] In fact, we have now reached a point where "issue and ideological concerns have become so important as a motivation for participation that party organizations are increasingly becoming 'issue-based networks of participatory activists'"[58] On the Republican side, the shift has been clearest in the growth of the influence of the Christian Right on the party,[59] while the Democrats have seen the growing influence of pro-choice, gay rights, and environmental organizations,[60] and a shift in the nature of the union movement with much greater strength and visibility among unions with agendas more similar than different from these other groups.[61] As a result, party activists have become more ideological than the electorate, with Republicans moving to the right and Democrats moving to the left.[62] This can be seen in a survey done by *The New York Times* in 2000 which found that 30 percent of Republican delegates to their national convention thought of themselves as "very conservative," compared to only 21 percent of Republican voters, while the percentage of Democratic delegates who considered themselves very liberal was 14 percent, compared to 6 percent of Democratic voters.[63] In some ways, this shift has also helped the parties to rebound from the low point of their strength in the 1960s and early 1970s, a period in which they were much more divided ideologically. The growing strength of these ideological, issue-based activist groups within the parties has led to more ideologically consistent and homogeneous parties. Jeffrey Stonecash's analysis of National Election Studies results, for example, found that the percentage of Republicans who identified themselves as conservatives increased from 47 percent in the 1970s to 49 percent in the 1980s to 57 percent in the 1990s. And looking at it from an alternative perspective, of those who identify as conservative, the percentage that also identified themselves as Republicans increased from 57 percent in the 1970s to 62 percent in the 1980s to 67 percent in the 1990s. And after factoring in a number of other issues and the positions the Republicans took, Stonecash concluded that "from the early 1960s to the 1990s, the Republican Party had moved from a relatively moderate and mixed-constituency party to one in which conservatives were of increasing importance."[64]

Similarly, though not quite so starkly, Stonecash found that the Democrats had moved in a liberal direction. The percentage of Democrats identifying themselves as liberal rose slightly, from 26 percent in the 1970s and 25 percent in the 1980s to 29 percent in the 1990s. On the other hand, those who thought of themselves as liberals were more tied to the Democrats, with 73 percent of liberals identifying as Democrats in the 1970s, 75 percent of them doing so in the 1980s, and 80 percent responding similarly in the 1990s. Thus, while there was more division between moderates and liberals in the Democratic Party than there was between moderates and conservatives in the Republican Party, and the Democratic Party was thus less ideologically homogeneous, the party had moved in a liberal direction, and the distinctions on an ideological level between it and the Republican Party had become clearer.[65]

As with the other changes involving money and consultants discussed above, this greater ideological clarity made it easier for the parties to operate internally, as fierce ideological differences are much less likely to emerge. On the other hand, it has made the parties seem less appealing to a more moderate general electorate (as will be documented below).

All of these trends, then, at least through the year 2000, led to a party system that was not attractive to the public. The large amounts of money that parties raised and distributed fed a sense that ordinary citizens did not matter to leaders. Parties and their leaders were seen as tied to big money, not the public. Voters were targets of marketing efforts, not mobilizing activities.

And the parties seemed to be ideologically strident in ways that made citizens feel disconnected from them. Parties, which used to play a role as organizations that linked citizens to the electoral process, were much less likely to succeed in that capacity, as can be seen by the well-documented decline of party identification and its impact on voter turnout.[66]

TABLE 5-6: Party Identification 7-Point Scale, 1952–2004

	St. Dem.	Weak Dem.	**Dem. (Tot)**	Ind. Dem.	Ind.	Ind. Rep.	**Ind. (Tot)**	Weak Rep.	St. Rep.	**Rep. (Tot)**
52	22	25	**47**	10	6	7	**23**	14	14	**28**
56	21	23	**44**	6	9	8	**23**	14	15	**29**
60	20	25	**45**	6	10	7	**23**	14	16	**30**
64	27	25	**52**	9	8	6	**23**	14	11	**25**
68	20	25	**45**	10	11	9	**30**	15	10	**25**
72	15	26	**41**	11	13	10	**34**	13	10	**23**
76	15	25	**40**	12	15	10	**37**	14	9	**23**
80	18	23	**41**	11	13	10	**34**	14	9	**23**
84	17	20	**37**	11	11	12	**34**	15	12	**27**
88	17	18	**35**	12	11	13	**36**	14	14	**28**
92	18	18	**36**	14	12	12	**38**	14	11	**25**
96	18	19	**37**	14	9	12	**35**	15	12	**27**
00	19	15	**34**	15	12	13	**40**	12	12	**24**
04	17	16	**33**	17	10	12	**39**	12	16	**28**

Figures are from the American National Election Study Guide to Public Opinion and Electoral Behavior. The Party Identification figures are at www.umich.edu /~nes/nesguide/toptable/tab2a_1.htm.

This decline occurred largely in the 1960s and 1970s when the percentage of independents grew and the percentage of strong partisans declined, as seen in table 5-6. Since then, there have been some ups and downs, but very little change. The number of independents has grown a small amount, as have the number of strong partisans.

Table 5-7, adapted and updated from a study by William Mayer, compares the average strength of partisanship in the three elections before this decline set in (1952–1960) with the three most recent elections (1996–2004) and the three elections prior to that (1984–1992).[67]

TABLE 5-7: Strength of Partisanship: Summary			
	1952–60 Avg.	1984–92 Avg.	1996–04 Avg.
Strong Partisans	36	30	32
Weak Partisans	38	33	30
Independent Leaners	15	25	28
Pure Independents	8	13	11
The table is adapted from table 5.8 in Mayer, William, "Mass Partisanship," in Shafer, Byron, ed., *Partisan Approaches to Postwar American Politics* (New York: Chatham House, 1998), p. 212. The figures are compiled from the American National Election Study Guide to Public Opinion and Electoral Behavior, Strength of Partisanship Table found at www.umich.edu/~nes/nesguide/toptable/tab2a_3.htm.			

TABLE 5-8: Voter Turnout by Partisan Groups, 1984–2004			
	Strong Partisans	Weak Partisans	Independent Leaners
1984	86%	72%	70%
1988	84%	69%	64%
1992	86%	75%	73%
1996	91%	74%	72%
2000	86%	72%	69%
2004	89%	78%	71%
Figures are self-reported voting turnout within each category of partisans. The data was compiled from the appropriate American National Election Study and was made available through the InterUniversity Consortium for Political and Social Research (ICPSR). In 2004, a split sample was asked different versions of the self-reporting vote turnout question. The figure reported here combines the two samples.			

It is true that partisan behavior has not changed as much as these figures might indicate, since independents who claim to lean toward one party or the other are as loyal to that party in their voting behavior as weak partisans.[68] However, that is a reflection—at least in part—of the limited choices that voters face in our two-party system. In most elections, voting for the Democrat or the Republican is the only choice that matters, so it should not be surprising that many who do not identify with one or the other of the major parties find themselves generally making one of those choices. And it is also the case, as table 5-8 documents, that these independents who lean toward one of the parties are less likely to vote than are partisans, though the differences with weak partisans, while consistent, are not particularly large.

TABLE 5-9: Perceptions of Party Differences, 1960–2004

	60	64	68	72	76	80	84	88	92	96	00	04
Difference	50	55	52	46	47	58	63	60	60	64	64	76

The figures are the percentage of respondents who say there is a difference between the two parties. They come from the American National Election Study Guide to Public Opinion and Electoral Behavior, Important Differences Between the Parties Table, found at www.umich.edu/~nes/ nesguide/toptable/tab2b_4.htm.

The loyalty of partisan voters and independent leaners, as we would expect, grows stronger as citizens perceive greater differences between the parties. Table 5-9 documents the growing difference that citizens perceive, and table 5-10 shows the corresponding small increase in the loyalty of partisan voters and independents who lean one way or another. But this increase in loyalty resulting from greater party differences does not mean there is greater satisfaction with the parties, as it has not been accompanied by an increase in those identifying with the parties. The number of independents remains stable and actually has crept up slightly in recent elections.[69] Voters are less, not more, satisfied with these "clear choices" that they face.

Some, most notably Morris Fiorina, have argued that the polarization of American voters is a myth.[70] And on one level, that is correct. Voters are not nearly as partisan and polarized as political elites and elected officials. Scott Keeter's analysis for the Pew Research Center of data from December 2004 found that the public was best divided into four different ideological categories, adding libertarians (social liberalism and economic conservatism) and populists (social conservatives and economic liberals) to liberals and conservatives, with almost half—42 percent—fitting into none of these categories. And he concludes that our public is best described as an "ideologically multipolar polity, with many ambivalent non-ideologues occupying a large middle ground."[71]

But the fact that our electoral system seems to be forcing us into this more polarized perspective, creating more clearly defined liberal Democratic and conservative Republican Parties, has divided, not united, the nation and helps lead to the dissatisfaction with the entire system that has been documented in these pages.[72] Voters do see increasingly clear choices, and by that measure, our politics is more polarized. But voters do not find the choices to reflect their less ideologically strong commitments. That is why candidates of the center—or who appeal to the center—are often popular, with John McCain being the clearest example in recent elections. But it is difficult for less partisan, more centrist candidates to win the party's nomination, and as the parties appear to be moving to the extreme, voters find it easier to choose, coming down more consistently on one side or the other (though they are not particularly happy with this choice). The candidates that these parties nominate for president are less and less acceptable.

TABLE 5-10: Loyalty of Partisan Voters, Summary Measures

	Avg. 1952–60	Avg. 1984–92	Avg. 1996-04
Strong Partisans	92%	95%	97%
Weak Partisans	75%	80%	86%
Independent Leaners	81%	88%	84%
Straight-Ticket Voting President-House	86%	76%	82%

Figures for partisan loyalty are based on the percentage of people who voted for their party's candidate for president. The 1952–1960 average was listed in Mayer, William, "Mass Partisanship," in Shafer, Byron, ed., *Partisan Approaches to Postwar American Politics*, table 5-8, p. 212. The 1984–1992 and 1996–2004 averages were computed from the American National Election Studies of the relevant years, with data made available through the InterUniversity Consortium for Political and Social Research. The straight-ticket voting figures are from the American National Election Study Guide to Public Opinion and Electoral Behavior Split Ticket Voting Table found at www.umich.edu/~nes/nesguide/toptable/tab9b_2.htm.

Tables 5-11 and 5-12 document this decreasing satisfaction in two different ways. Since 1968, the American National Election Study has been asking people to place the candidates on a "feeling thermometer" scale that measures how warmly or coldly they feel about the candidates. If we look at the highest feeling thermometer rating for either the Democratic or Republican candidate, we see a small but steady trend of decline. In 1968 and 1972,

Richard Nixon received thermometer ratings of 66, the highest given to presidential candidates in this era, and—with the exception of a drop to 56 in 1980, a rating given to both Carter and Reagan in that year—there was always at least one candidate who scored above 60 in each election through 1988. Since then, the highest-rated candidate has never been above the 59 that Clinton received in 1996, and in 2004 neither candidate was higher than 55 (the rating for Bush; Kerry was at 53).

TABLE 5-11: Feeling Thermometer Average of Most Popular Candidate, 1968–2004

Election Year	68	72	76	80	84	88	92	96	00	04
Feeling Thermometer	66	66	63	56	61	60	56	59	57	55
Most Pop. Candidate.	R	R	D	T	R	R	D	D	D	R

The figure is the highest average feeling thermometer score for the Democratic or Republican candidate for president in each election year, and the party of that candidate (T = tied ratings). The data was taken from the American National Election Study Guide to Public Opinion and Electoral Behavior. The table with feeling thermometer averages can be found at www.umich.edu/~nes/nesguide/toptable/tab7a_2.htm.

Similarly, these studies have been asking citizens in open-ended questions to name things they liked or disliked about the major candidates. If we take the net score for each candidate (the number of positive comments minus the number of negative comments) and compute the average across all citizens, we see that the more popular of the two candidates has gotten less popular over time. In the first four elections in the time series, the more popular of the two candidates had an average of close to or more than one more positive than negative comment from citizens. From 1968 through 1976, this average dropped to between 0.3 and 0.5 more positive comments, and since 1980 (the lowest point in the time series when both candidates averaged more negative than positive comments), only Bill Clinton in 1992 had an average above 0.2, with 2004 displaying the second lowest total in the series—John Kerry had on average equal numbers of positive and negative comments. (President Bush had on average slightly more negative than positive comments, with an average of -0.3.) We are increasingly unhappy with the choices we face in presidential elections. And this is one trend that did not reverse itself in 2004.

TABLE 5-12: Like-Dislike Net Responses for Most-Liked Presidential Candidate, 1952–2004			
	Highest Likes- Dislikes Average		Highest Likes- Dislikes Average
1952	1.0 (R)	1980	-0.2 (D)
1956	1.2 (R)	1984	0.0 (T)
1960	0.9 (R)	1988	0.1 (R)
1964	1.0 (D)	1992	0.4 (D)
1968	0.4 (R)	1996	0.2 (D)
1972	0.5 (R)	2000	0.2 (D)
1976	0.3 (D)	2004	0.0 (D)

The number is the higher of the two averages taking the number of likes minus the number of dislikes mentioned in the open-ended question of whether there was anything the respondent liked or disliked about each of the candidates. Up to five likes or dislikes were coded, with the party of the candidate with a better average like-to-dislike figure noted (T= the candidates were tied). The data was in the American National Election Study Guide to Public Opinion and Electoral Behavior. The table with this data is at www.umich.edu/~nes/nesguide/toptable/tab7a_1.htm.

Perhaps at some point, as Stonecash argues, voters will find these choices more acceptable and begin to identify with one of the parties more fully and with the system more broadly.[73] Party identification figures and feelings about the candidates in 2004 indicate that this has not yet happened, although as we have seen many of the other trends I have documented here—most visibly voter turnout, but other patterns as well—did seem to reverse themselves in 2004, pointing to a more involved electorate. In the final chapter of this work, we need to take a closer look at 2004, examining which of these changes may reflect longer-term, healthier democratic trends and which seem election-specific and not likely to hold up over time. This will allow us to conclude with an examination of what, if anything, we might do to reconnect the public with our democratic process.

Notes

1 For a good recent summary of these trends, see Rosenstone, Steven, and Hansen, John Mark, *Mobilization, Participation and Democracy in America* (New York: Longman,

2003).

2 Brody, Richard, "The Puzzle of Political Participation in America," in King, Anthony, ed., *The New American Political System* (Washington, DC: The American Enterprise Institute, 1978).

3 The data are from the American National Election Study, 2004, and can be found at their website at: http://www.umich.edu/~nes/nesguide/2ndtable/t6a_2_2.htm. Note that these figures are much higher than the voter turnout figures in table 5-1. That is because the ANES relies on self-reported voting. This overestimates the percentage of voters in two ways. Non-voters are undersampled, and people overreport voting. If anything, these figures, then, underestimate the differences based on education, since less-educated citizens are more likely to overreport voting and less likely to be sampled.

4 Wolfinger, Raymond, and Rosenstone, Steven, *Who Votes* (New Haven, CT: Yale University Press, 1980). For a discussion of the strong relationship of education to participation in a variety of activities and in a variety of places, see the work of Sidney Verba with a variety of co-authors. The basic theory defining the importance of socio-economic status—and, thus, education—to participation was outlined in Verba, Sidney, and Nie, Norman, *Participation in America* (New York: Harper & Row, 1972). This work was expanded to explore other democracies in Verba, Sidney; Nie, Norman; and Kim, Jae-On, *Participation and Political Equality* (Cambridge: Cambridge University Press, 1978). The strongest statement of the way that this relationship operates can be found in Verba, Sidney; Schlozman, Kay; and Brady, Henry, *Voice and Equality* (Cambridge, MA: Harvard University Press, 1995). And the specific way it has impacted gender differences in participation is explored in Burns, Nancy; Schlozman, Kay; and Verba, Sidney, *The Private Roots of Public Action* (Cambridge, MA: Harvard University Press, 2001). There is also a good summary discussion of this relationship in Conway, Margaret, *Political Participation in the United States*, 3rd ed. (Washington, DC: CQ Press, 2000).

5 In addition to Rosenstone and Hansen, a good discussion of this aspect of voter turnout can be found in Hill, David Lee, *American Voter Turnout: An Institutional Perspective* (Boulder, CO: Westview Press, 2006). And for an earlier examination of this issue, see Piven, Frances Fox, and Cloward, Richard, *Why Americans Don't Vote* (New York: Pantheon Books, 1988).

6 See Teixeira, Rudy, *The Disappearing American Voter* (Washington, DC: Brookings Institution, 1992), ch. 4.

7 These figures are taken from table 9.1 on page 207 of Valelly, Richard, *The Two Reconstructions* (Chicago: University of Chicago Press, 2004), the best examination of the struggle for achieving voting rights for African Americans.

8 Rosenstone and Hansen, *Mobilization, Participation and Democracy in America*, 222, and table 7.2, 220.

9 See *Oregon* v. *Mitchell*, 400 U.S. 112 (1970).

10 See *Marston* v. *Lewis*, 410 U.S. 679 (1973).

11 Rosenstone and Hansen, *Mobilization, Participation and Democracy in America*, 208.

12 Brians, Craig, and Grofman, Bernard, "Election Day Registration's Effect on U.S. Voter Turnout," *Social Science Quarterly* 82 (2001): 170–83. Also see their earlier paper on the

topic using data from the three states with long-standing Election Day registration, "When Election Barriers Fall," *Public Choice* 99 (1999): 161–76.

13 Ansolabehere, Stephen, and Konisky, David, "The Introduction of Voter Registration and Its Effect on Turnout," *Political Analysis* 14 (2006): 83–100.

14 Rosenstone and Hansen, *Mobilization, Participation and Democracy in America*, 208.

15 See Hill, *American Voter Turnout*, and Conway, *Political Participation in the United States*.

16 See Oliver, J. Eric, "The Effect of Eligibility Restrictions and Party Activity on Absentee Voting and Overall Turnout," *American Journal of Political Science* 40 (1996): 498–513.

17 The most comprehensive studies of the impact of mail voting (and, by implication, other forms of early voting) on turnout indicate that it might not be as strong as some of its proponents argue, but it does nonetheless have a positive impact on turnout. See Karp, Jeffrey, and Banducci, Susan, "Going Postal: How All-Mail Elections Influence Turnout," *Political Behavior* 22 (2000): 223–39.

18 The strongest challenge to this view came from a study done by the Committee for the Study of the American Electorate, *Two Pro-Participation Reforms Actually Harm Voter Turnout: Other Reforms Suggested* (Washington, DC: Committee for the Study of the American Electorate, 2001). This study noted that when turnout went up in 2000, states that had adopted some of these reforms saw a smaller increase in voter turnout than did states that did not, and that in the 1996 election cycle states that had adopted these reforms saw a larger decrease than states that did not. However, the study did find that the initial effect of adoption of these reforms was to increase turnout, but that in the long run, that increase did not hold. But that suggests that the reforms do work, since making it easier to vote does lead to more people voting. What happens, however, is that the increases are relatively small, and that means that when the forces that have led to continuing declines in participation overpower these gains, the disillusionment may be even stronger. And this suggests that the answer will depend on more than these simple structural reforms.

19 States with Election Day registration were exempted from this mail-in provision, which was one reason for the jump in the number of states allowing Election Day registration in the mid-1990s.

20 Conway, *Political Participation in America*, 120–22. The quotation is from p. 122.

21 McDonald, Michael, and Popkin, Samuel, "The Myth of the Vanishing Voter," *American Political Science Review* 95 (2001): 963–74.

22 Because their figures show less of a drop from 1972 through 2000, McDonald's figures also show a smaller increase in 2004. He estimates voter turnout in 2004 to have been 60 percent. See McDonald, Michael P., "Up, Up and Away! Voter Participation in the 2004 Presidential Election," *The Forum* 2:4 (2004), article 4, available at http://www.bepress.com/forum/vol2/ iss4/art4.

23 See Patterson, Thomas, *The Vanishing Voter* (New York: Alfred A. Knopf, 2002), 8–11.

24 The turnout among eligible voters outside the South dropped from over 70 percent in 1960 to 60 percent by 1972, and to just over 50 percent in 1996. See Patterson, 9.

25 Patterson, *The Vanishing Voter*, 10.

26 Doppelt, Jack, and Shearer, Ellen, *Non-Voters: America's No Shows* (Thousand Oaks,

CA: Sage, 1999), cited in Patterson, 10.

27 Norris, Pippa, *Count Every Voice: Democratic Participation Worldwide* (New York: Cambridge University Press, 2002).

28 See the Sentencing Project, "Felony Disenfranchisement Laws in the United States," http://www.sentencingproject.org/pubs_05.cfm.

29 See Putnam, Robert, "Bowling Alone," *Journal of Democracy* 6 (1995): 65–78; *Bowling Alone: The Collapse and Renewal of American Community* (New York: Simon and Schuster, 2000); and *Democracies in Flux: The Evolution of Social Capital in Contemporary Society* (Oxford: Oxford University Press, 2002).

30 Putnam, Robert, "The Strange Disappearance of Civic America," *American Prospect* 24 (Winter 1996): 34.

31 Rosenstone and Hansen, *Mobilization, Participation and Democracy in America*, ch. 4. The quotation is from p. 126.

32 Putnam, Robert, "Bowling Together," *American Prospect*, 12 February 2002, 20–22.

33 See Skocpol, Theda, *Diminished Democracy* (Norman: University of Oklahoma Press, 2003), 11.

34 See Skocpol, Theda, and Fiorina, Morris, eds., *Civic Engagement in American Democracy* (Washington, DC: Brookings Institution, 1999).

35 Skocpol, *Diminished Democracy*, 174.

36 Dalton, Russell, *Citizen Politics*, 4th ed. (Washington, DC: CQ Press, 2006), 47–50. The quotations are both from p. 50.

37 Hansen, John Mark, "The Majoritarian Influence and the Declining Significance of Place," in Pomper, Gerald, and Weiner, Mark, eds., *The Future of American Democratic Politics* (New Brunswick, NJ: Rutgers University Press, 2003), 39–54. The quotation is from p. 47.

38 Rutenberg, Jim, "The 2004 Campaign; First Debate Draws Large TV Audience," *The New York Times,* 2 October 2004. Found in *The New York Times* on-line archives.

39 The Nielsen data, aside from the audience figures for the first debates in 1996 and 2000, which is referenced in note 38 above, is all cited in Patterson, *The Vanishing Voter*, 15. Patterson also documents the declining audience for presidential primary debates and the national conventions on p. 16.

40 See Rutenberg, "The 2004 Campaign," and Stanley, Alessandra, "The 2004 Campaign: On Television: Bush Smiles, but Laughter Falls Short," *The New York Times*, 14 October 2004. Found in *The New York Times* on-line archives.

41 For more extended discussion of the issue of declining trust in government and its implications, see Miller, Arthur, "Political Issues and Trust in Government: 1964–1970," *American Political Science Review* 68 (1974): 951–72; Citrin, Jack, "Comment: The Political Relevance of Trust in Government," *American Political Science Review* 68 (1974): 973–88; Lipset, Seymour Martin, and Schneider, William, *The Confidence Gap* (Baltimore: Johns Hopkins University Press, 1987); Lipset, Seymour Martin, and Schneider, William, "The Confidence Gap During the Reagan Years, 1981–1987," *Political Science Quarterly* 102 (1987): 1–23; Abramson, Paul, *Political Attitudes in America* (San Francisco: W.H. Freeman, 1983); Tolchin, Susan, *The Angry American*, 2nd ed. (Boulder, CO: Westview Press, 1989); and Cappella, Joseph, and Jamieson, Kathleen Hall, *The*

Spiral of Cynicism (New York: Oxford University Press, 1997).

42 Conway, *Political Participation in the United States*, 172.

43 The literature here is enormous. For example, see Wattenberg, Martin, *The Decline of American Political Parties, 1952–1994* (Cambridge, MA: Harvard University Press, 1996); or Menfee-Libey, David, *The Triumph of Campaign-Centered Politics* (New York: Chatham House, 2000).

44 Bibby, John, "Party Organizations, 1946–1996," in Shafer, Byron, ed., *Partisan Approaches to Postwar American Politics* (New York: Chatham House, 1998), 142–85. The quotation appears on p. 174.

45 See also Cotter, Cornelius; Gibson, James; Bibby, John; and Huckshorn, Robert, *Party Organizations in American Politics* (New York: Praeger, 1984); Frantzich, Stephen, *Political Parties in the Technological Age* (New York: Longman, 1989); and Maisel, L. Sandy, *Parties and Elections in America*, 2nd ed. (New York: McGraw-Hill, 1993).

46 Bibby, "Party Organizations," 177.

47 In *Buckley* v. *Valeo*, 421 U.S. 1 (1976), the Supreme Court ruled that the law imposes "independent reporting requirements on individuals and groups that are not candidates or political committees only in the following circumstances: (1) when they make contributions earmarked for political purposes or authorized or requested by a candidate or his agent, to some person other than a candidate or political committee, and (2) when they make expenditures for communications that expressly advocate the election or defeat of a clearly identified candidate."

48 According to the Court, in fn. 52 of the Buckley case, express advocacy applied "to communications containing express words of advocacy of election or defeat, such as "vote for," "elect," "support," "cast your ballot for," "Smith for Congress," "vote against," "defeat," "reject." That list of words and phrases became known as the "magic words," and as long as ads steered clear of using them, they could pretty much say anything they wanted and not be considered to "express advocacy." This led, for example, to many supportive ads asking citizens to "thank" a person rather than "vote for" her or him.

49 Abramson, Jill, "Campaign Finance: Audit Faults Clinton and Dole Ads," *The New York Times*, 11 December 1998, A1, A24.

50 Herrnson, Paul, "Reemergent National Party Organizations," in Maisel, L. Sandy, ed., *The Parties Respond* (Boulder, CO: Westview Press, 1990), 51.

51 See Sabato, Larry, *The Rise of Political Consultants: New Ways of Winning Elections* (New York: Basic Books, 1981).

52 See the data cited by Dulio, David, *For Better or Worse: How Political Consultants Are Changing Elections in the United States* (Albany: State University of New York Press, 2004), esp. ch. 5.

53 See Kolodny, Robin, "Electoral Partnerships: Political Consultants and Political Parties," in Thurber, James, and Nelson, Candice, eds., *Campaign Warriors: The Role of Political Consultants in Elections* (Washington, DC: Brookings Institution Press, 2000), ch. 7. Also, Kolodny, Robin, and Logan, Angela, "Political Consultants and the Extension of Party Goals," *PS: Political Science and Politics* 31 (1998): 155–59.

54 Dulio, David, and Nelson, Candice, *Vital Signs* (Washington, DC: Brookings Institution

Press, 2005), 50–51.

55 Kolodny, "Electoral Partnerships," 129.

56 *Eldred* v. *Burns*, 427 U.S. 347 (1976).

57 For an early discussion of the switch from professional- to amateur-dominated parties, see Wilson, James Q., *The Amateur Democrat* (Chicago: University of Chicago Press, 1966). In addition, one can see this shift in Samuel Eldersveld's studies of activists in Detroit politics, which find over time an increasing number of activists who are motivated by their desire to work on issues. For a summary, see Eldersveld, Samuel, and Walton, Hanes, Jr., *Political Parties in American Society*, 2nd ed. (Boston: Bedford/St. Martin's, 2000), ch. 8.

58 Shafer, Byron, ed., *Postwar Politics in the G-7: Orders and Eras in Comparative Perspective* (Madison: University of Wisconsin Press, 1996), 36, quoted in Bibby, John, *Politics, Parties, and Elections in America*, 5th ed. (Belmont, CA: Wadsworth/Thomas Learning, 2003), 143.

59 See Wilcox, Clyde, *Onward Christian Soldiers: The Religious Right in American Politics* (Boulder, CO: Westview Press, 1996).

60 Bibby, John, "Party Organizations, 1946–1996," in Shafer, *Partisan Approaches to Postwar American Politics*. See also Berry, Jeffrey, *The New Liberalism* (Washington, DC: Brookings Institution Press, 1999), for a discussion of the changing nature of liberal interest groups.

61 Shafer, Byron, "Partisan Elites, 1946–1996," in Shafer, *Partisan Approaches to Postwar American Politics*.

62 Miller, Warren, and Jennings, Kent, *Parties in Transition: A Longitudinal Study of Party Elites and Supporters* (New York: Russell Sage Foundation, 1988).

63 *The New York Times*, 17 August 2000, A17.

64 Stonecash, Jeffrey, *Class and Party in American Politics* (Boulder, CO: Westview Press, 2000), 64–66. The quotation is from p. 66.

65 Stonecash, *Class and Party in American Politics*, 78–80.

66 See, for example, Wattenberg, Martin, *The Decline of American Political Parties: 1952–1994* (Cambridge, MA: Harvard University Press, 1996), and *Where Have All the Voters Gone* (Cambridge, MA: Harvard University Press, 2002); or Abramowitz, Alan, *Voice of the People* (Boston: McGraw-Hill, 2004).

67 See Mayer, William, "Mass Partisanship," in Shafer, *Partisan Approaches to Postwar American Politics*, ch 5.

68 For the strongest argument in favor of this assertion, see Keith, Bruce, et al., *The Myth of the Independent Voter* (Berkeley: University of California Press, 1992).

69 Jeffrey Stonecash makes the argument that the clearer difference between the parties reflects the end stage of a long-term secular realignment and that voter loyalties to the parties and the system will follow. But he notes that one measure that has not reversed itself from the 1970s is the percentage of independents in the electorate. And he underestimates the importance of that measure as a testament to party strength, as that is one measure where voters are not forced into a choice between the two major parties but can opt out if they want to do so. The behavior of party loyalty and less split-ticket voting that he documents does reflect important changes in the electoral system, but as the evi-

dence presented here suggests, this greater partisan division results in less, not more, voter satisfaction. See Stonecash, Jeffrey, *Political Parties Matter: Realignment and the Return of Partisan Voting* (Boulder, CO: Lynne Rienner Publishers, 2006).

70 See Fiorina, Morris, *Culture War? The Myth of a Polarized America*, 2nd ed. (New York: Pearson Longman, 2006).

71 Keeter, Scott, "In Search of Ideologues in America: It's Harder Than You May Think," a poll analysis from the Pew Research Center that can be found at http://pewresearch.org/obdeck/?ObDeckID=17, 11 April 2006. Also see Pew Research Center, *Mapping the Political Landscape 2005* (Washington, DC: The Pew Research Center, 2005). This study does find a relatively polarized nation, but one characterized by as much division within the party coalitions as between the parties, leading to their sorting the electorate into nine different groups.

72 For what seems to be a contrary view from the "myth of polarization" view just described, arguing that the nation is in fact polarized, see Jacobson, Gary, *A Divider, Not a Uniter: George Bush and the American People* (New York: Pearson Longman, 2007). If the argument in these pages is correct, both Jacobson and Fiorina are also correct, as they are simply exploring different aspects of the same dynamic. Voters are in some ways less polarized than our political system seems to be illustrating, but that is because we have, in partisan terms, become more polarized, and this is a source of frustration and disgust for many.

73 Stonecash, Jeffrey, *Political Parties Matter*. Chapter 8.

CHAPTER 6

The 2004 Election and Prospects for the Future: Reclaiming Democratic Control

The 2004 presidential election provided some basis for hope that the disconnect between the public and our electoral process and the decline of democracy may have begun to reverse itself. As we have seen, many of the trends measuring citizen satisfaction with and participation in our democratic processes, which had shown a steady decline since the 1960s, showed strong reversals. The most prominent was the rise in voter turnout to levels not seen since 1972, but there were other hopeful trends as well. A larger percentage of money raised by the candidates came from small contributions, the type of contribution least likely to fuel cynicism and alienation. More people paid attention to the campaign and watched the debates and other events. And the grass-roots activities of both parties and other groups were, at least in some places, extensive.

But in other ways, there was still evidence of a continuing alienation from the system. People were still dissatisfied with the campaign and still felt as if they did not have much say in what was happening. There was no change in party identification. And people were still dissatisfied with the choices that they were presented with. Furthermore, there had been elections since the 1960s where many of the trends documented previously had reversed themselves temporarily—particularly in 1984 and 1992—as a result of the particular context of those elections, only to find the negative trends resuming shortly thereafter.

In this final chapter, then, we need to take a closer look at the 2004 election and which trends, if any, seem to hold hope for rebuilding a stronger democratic culture, and which, by contrast, seem to be the result of election-specific factors that are unlikely to stand the test of time. And this will allow us, finally, to take a closer look at what changes we might try to institute in order to build upon those hopeful trends, reverse others, and reclaim our electoral process.

The 2004 Election

There are already many accounts of the 2004 election, and it is not necessary here to provide a descriptive overview of all that happened in that election.[1] Rather, I want to focus here on the factors that may have led to greater involvement by citizens in that election. And clearly, the most important factor here was the expected closeness of the election. The 2000 election had been remarkably close, with Al Gore actually winning the popular vote by half a million votes while losing the Electoral College by the narrowest of margins, after the disputed Florida election was officially certified as having been won by George W. Bush. And in the early days of the Bush presidency there was no reason to believe that the evenly divided nature of the electorate was going to change very much, as the president's approval ratings hovered in the mid-50s (see table 6-1). After the terrorist attacks of September 11, 2001, those ratings saw the largest "rally" ever recorded,[2] spiking to levels above 90 percent. But that moment of unity began to fade away, and in spite of brief jumps in support after particular events (such as the invasion of Iraq, the capture of Saddam Hussein, and the holding of elections in Iraq), the president's approval fell into a pattern of steady decline. By the time of the 2004 election, his approval ratings were at a level where there was every expectation that the closeness of 2000 would be repeated in 2004.

Thus the public, the press, and the participants (candidates, parties, and groups) all expected that the outcome might hinge on a small number of votes. And since there were clear differences between the parties reflecting the movement of party elites into a more polarized structure (documented in chapter 5), the sense that this election would matter was relatively strong. This led to both greater citizen involvement as more felt that they might make a difference, and greater grass-roots activity by parties and other groups to mobilize citizens and get them to the polls, as candidates and parties took to heart the research that had been done by Donald Green and Alan Gerber on the importance of direct contact in raising voter turnout.[3] Table 6-2 shows that the increase in turnout was greater in those states targeted by the parties, with much smaller increases coming in those states not projected to be close. And it was not just the parties. Groups, especially on the Democratic side, such America Coming Together (ACT) and Moveon.org also engaged in strong voter mobilization campaigns.[4] And a study by Bergan, Gerber, Green, and Panagopoulos attributed about one-third of the increase in voter turnout to mobilization activities, with most of the increase resulting from citizens seeing the election as important and close.[5]

TABLE 6-1: Approval Ratings for President George W. Bush

	Pew Approval	NY Times/ CBS Approval		Pew Approval	NY Times/ CBS Approval
Feb. 2001	53	53	Nov. 2003	50	50
May 2001	53	57	Feb. 2004	48	47
Aug. 2001	50	50	May 2004	44	41
Nov. 2001	84	86	Aug. 2004	46	46
Feb. 2002	78	78	Nov. 2004	48	51
May 2002	70	71	Feb. 2005	46	49
Aug. 2002	67	66	May 2005	43	46
Nov. 2002	61	65	Aug. 2005	40	41
Feb. 2003	54	54	Nov. 2005	36	40
May 2003	65	67	Feb. 2006	40	34
Aug. 2003	56	55	May 2006	36	31

Numbers are percentage of respondents to the Pew Research Center and *New York Times*/CBS News polls who approved of the job President Bush was doing. If no poll was taken in the month (chosen for quarterly ratings), then the next available poll result was listed. For the Pew results, May 2002 poll is from June, November 2002 poll is from December, November 2004 poll is from December, August 2005 poll is from September, and May 2004 poll is from July. For the *New York Times*/CBS News results November 2001 poll is from December, and November 2005 result is from December. If more than one poll was conducted in the given month, I used the one closest to the middle of the month.

The Pew figures are from the report *Dubai Ports Fallout: Bush Approval Falls to 33%, Congress Earns Rare Praise*, 15 March 2006, p. 11, and the final figure is from "Americans' Support for Israel Unchanged by Recent Hostilities," 26 July 2006, both available for download at their website, http://people-press.org.

The *New York Times* figures are from The Complete Poll Results of the *New York Times*/CBS News poll, released 27 July 2006, p. 2, available for download at http://www.nytimes.com/2006/07/27/washington/27poll.html `?ex=1155182400&en=50c03f9fdc38b948&ei=5070.

TABLE 6-2: Turnout Increase, 2000–2004, by Level of State Targeting		
	Turnout Increase: VAP	Turnout Increase: Citizen VAP
Not Targeted (28 states)	+2.6%	+3.5%
Partially Targeted (14 states)	+4.2%	+5.1%
Fully Targeted (9 states)	+6.3%	+6.5%

Figures are the average (mean) change in turnout among the states and District of Columbia from 2000 to 2004 computed using both the voting age population (VAP) and population estimates excluding non-citizens. (See chapter 5 for a discussion of the dispute over which figures present a more accurate picture of turnout.) The state turnout figures come from table A-5: Reported Voting and Registration for Total and Citizen Voting-Age Population by State as Compiled by the U.S. Census Bureau, Current Population Report, released on-line on 26 May 2005 at www.census.gov/population/www/socdemo/voting/cps2004.html.

Fully Targeted are those states that were on both parties' list the entire campaign; Partially Targeted were on the list of at least one of the parties for at least part of the campaign; Not Targeted (which includes the District of Columbia) were not on either party's list at any time during the campaign.

The question, then, is whether or not these factors can help build long-term connections between citizens and our democratic system. And here the answer is mixed. It seems likely that the close divide of the public will remain at least through 2008. The Republicans may have had an opportunity to build a more permanent majority after the events of 9/11, but that opportunity has disappeared. And whoever wins the election of 2008 may have a similar opportunity—and current short-term forces favor the Democrats here—but as Green, Palmquist, and Schickler remind us, and the figures cited in chapter 5 make clear, partisanship changes slowly. It "induces a powerful central tendency in election outcomes, dampening the electoral effects of short-term forces and causing deviant election outcomes to return to the norm."[6] In other words, the relatively even divide between the parties is likely to remain in place for quite some time, changing slowly as the result of longer-term demographic and structural changes, perhaps sped up (or delayed) by the perception that one party is particularly effective in meeting the short-term issues and concerns that do arise.[7] This means we are likely to continue to have close presidential elections, raising the level of citizen concern and interest. And this will also provide continued incentive for parties to focus on grass-roots mobilization. While it may be true that most of the increase in turnout in 2004 was due to citizen interest and not mobilization,

> mobilization strategies provide campaigns with relatively dependable returns on their investments. Unlike television ads or new policy announcements, creating a grassroots infrastructure is almost certain to pay dividends in terms of votes. The rate of return is probably much smaller than that of a highly successful ad campaign but also less risky. From that standpoint, the 2004 election may prove to be a turning point in the investment portfolios of presidential campaigns. Whereas previous campaigns tended to invest the preponderance of their resources in persuasive communication, campaigns operating in an era of partisan parity may be gravitating toward the small but steady returns of grassroots activity.[8]

Citizens, then, are likely to see close elections that matter, and parties are likely to have incentives to continue grass-roots mobilizing. And while some of the groups that formed to mobilize on the Democratic side, such as ACT, disbanded after the 2004 election, others, such as Moveon.org, remain committed to grass-roots organizing. Leading up to the 2006 elections, Moveon was organizing at the grass-roots level, with staff on the ground in ten states and a web-based campaign hooking volunteers together all across the nation.[9] Similarly, Howard Dean's 2004 campaign organization became the group Democracy for America, dedicated to "rebuild[ing] the Democratic Party from the bottom up," endorsing progressive Democrats in primaries and general elections, and mobilizing for them at the grass-roots level.[10] Thus, an environment is likely to exist that may help bring people into the system.

On the other hand, the strong partisanship of party elites and strong polarization of the parties is also likely to continue, and that, as we have seen, causes people to feel alienated from the system, since the public is not as ideologically coherent and divided as the electoral choices that are often seen. And the importance of money is likely to continue to grow, leading to further concern that the views of ordinary citizens do not matter and resulting in citizens pulling away from any kind of democratic commitment. The challenge, then, is to strengthen the forces that connect citizens while weakening the forces that lead us to sever our ties with politics.

Reclaiming Democracy: The Nomination Process

As we have seen, the most serious problem with the nomination process is the fact that for many citizens their participation does not seem to matter. The nominee is decided before they even begin paying much attention. And this situation has become worse over time as the process has become more front-loaded. Thus, the key to improving the process is to slow it down. But that is not likely to be easy. States have incentives to hold primaries sooner, rather than later, as that maximizes the chances that one's own state will make a difference and will get the kind of attention and influence that seems to come to Iowa and New Hampshire every four years. And, thus, the major effort underway is to move states up in the process. The Democrats, in fact, are tinkering with their calendar in order to put a second caucus in place between Iowa and New Hampshire, and yet another primary in place shortly after New Hampshire. The goal here is to add states that are "more representative" of the diversity of the Democratic Party than Iowa and New Hampshire—two states that are predominantly Caucasian but at the same time small enough to encourage the kind of retail politics that defines their primaries. The specific proposal would add Nevada, a state with a large Latino population, between Iowa and New Hampshire, and South Carolina, a state with a large African American population, after New Hampshire.[11] But while this proposal does add to the number of states that might provide a strong retail politics experience and, thus, an opportunity for inclusive and democratically satisfying experiences, it also exacerbates the front-loading problem. It squeezes the early calendar even more, leaving less time after Iowa before the next test, and less time after New Hampshire as well. And this will put a premium on the ability of candidates to have money in place before these contests begin in order to be able to take advantage of the opportunities these states will provide.

Furthermore, by front-loading the calendar even more, this proposal is likely to increase, not decrease, the importance of the first state on the calendar, Iowa, as there is less time to rebuild (for candidates who do "less well than expected") or falter (for candidates who do "much better than expected") before the next test. And this increases the likelihood that, from a national perspective, more citizens will feel that they have no influence over who their party nominates for president. While nothing is certain, given the multiple variables that go into the specific dynamic in any given election year, this proposal actually is likely to increase the chances that what happens in Iowa will seal the fate of most, if not all, of the candidates running for the nomination, as happened in 2004. Spreading things out, not compressing them, is the way to allow more citizens the opportunity to feel as if they can make a difference and thus motivate them to play a role in the nomination process.

Most of the other reforms in the calendar that have been suggested are also likely to fail. As noted in chapter 2, having a single national primary would theoretically maximize the number of citizens who "count," but such a primary would require enormous sums of money in order to be competitive, creating campaigns that are national, media-oriented, and cash-driven, precisely the kinds of campaigns least likely to draw people into the system. The retail experience of Iowa and New Hampshire would be lost. And proposals for regional primaries/caucuses suffer from the same problem, even if not quite as severely. While there would be more time to build a campaign as the votes of different regions are counted, allowing candidates more time to raise the resources and create the organizations they need, within each region the "big prizes"—the ones where the most delegates and most television and media focus—are going to be the largest states. Again, retail politics matters less; more alienating, cash-driven politics matters more. A series of regional primaries/caucuses would be much better than a national primary but is unlikely, on its own, to improve the situation.

There are, however, two suggested reforms that might help. The first is a proposal that was suggested by a Republican Party commission headed by former Tennessee Senator and Republican National Committee Chairman William Brock, which investigated the issue of the timing of the nomination campaign prior to the 2000 election. This plan, often referred to as the Delaware Plan (as it was first proposed by the Delaware delegation on the Brock Commission), would have set up a series of primaries beginning on March 1 and continuing once a month for four months. The time of a state's primary would have been determined by its size. The smallest states (Delaware, New Hampshire, the Dakotas, Wyoming, etc.) would have come first. The largest states (California, New York, Texas, Florida, etc.) would have come last.[12] This plan seemed likely to pass until it was killed by nominee George W. Bush in an attempt to keep the convention free of fighting and because of a concern that this change might also help the Democrats.[13] The other concern (and the reason that this might have caused a fight at the convention) was that many of the big states would have felt, as noted by Thomas Patterson, that candidates who won the earlier, smaller primaries would still have been anointed the winners even if they did not have enough delegates to have formally won the nomination, effectively leaving them out of the process.[14] So while a proposal (or something similar to it, particularly one that left Iowa and New Hampshire in their current slots and then began this process on March 1) has much to recommend it, especially in its ability to encourage grass-roots, retail campaigning and limit the importance of money and media, the likelihood of succeeding in establishing such a calendar is limited.

Perhaps a more likely, though still a difficult proposal to pass, would be a system based on a series of regional primaries spread monthly throughout the calendar but retaining the Iowa - New Hampshire start and lengthening the time between New Hampshire and the first regional primary. This would retain the grass-roots advantage of two early, small states (and one could even consider adding a couple of other small states early on as the new Democratic plan for 2008 does, so long as they are spread out a bit more) and provide time for candidates to build on that small-state experience before having to move into more expensive regional contests. To further entice states to accept this plan, the order of the regions would need to rotate so that no single region would always matter more, either based on a fixed schedule set four or five elections at a time or, even better, based on a random selection conducted a year before the election. But the impact of this reform is still likely to be limited by the fact, noted above, that the focus will probably be on the largest, most media-intensive states in the region. Furthermore, it is difficult to imagine such a reform passing in a practical sense, since the parties find it in their interest to choose their candidate as rapidly as possible. From a party's perspective, there is no scenario worse than fighting a long, drawn-out battle while the other side wraps things up quickly. Thus, parties resist reforms that may spread things out "too much." Shifting the calendar to improve citizen involvement in the process seems unlikely to occur. A more rational, fairly spaced calendar is worth fighting for, but not worth a major effort. Changes in finance laws and other strategies concerning the general election are more likely to be implemented, though even in that area, as we shall see, change will not be easy.

Reclaiming the Process: Increasing Competition

As we saw in chapter 4, one of the factors that weakens the connections that citizens feel with their government is the way in which changes in technology have made it easier for candidates to target their campaign based on a state-by-state Electoral College strategy. This means that the number of citizens who feel their vote will matter and the number mobilized is minimized. One way to solve this problem would be to eliminate or reform the Electoral College. But as was made clear earlier, the two ways that seem possible for reform—constitutional amendment or states changing from winner-take-all systems on their own—are unlikely at best. Thus, alternative strategies are needed. One such strategy is a plan to use a state-by-state approach to create a national change and create a *de facto* national popular election while leaving the machinery of the Electoral College in place. The plan, promoted by a group called National Popular Vote, would create an interstate pact wherein states would agree to cast their electoral votes for the candidate who wins the popular vote nationally. Not all states would need to join: only enough to add up to 270 electoral votes. Once that occurred, the popular vote winner would be guaranteed an electoral vote majority.[15] Bills committing states to join such a compact have been introduced in a number of states including New York, Arizona, and Colorado, and in California a bill passed the assembly and is out of committee in the state senate.[16] This effort attempts to take advantage of popular support for direct election of the president by offering a way to achieve this goal that falls within the boundaries of the U.S. Constitution. But there are limits as well. Most important, not only is it difficult to get state legislatures to deal with such issues, but it is also the case that many states find that the current system maximizes their influence. The states that serve to achieve the most immediate benefits from such a change are large states that are dominated by one of the parties, states such as California, New York, or Texas. Such states currently see much less campaign activity than their population size would seem to dictate, and a switch to a national popular vote would see much greater emphasis on appealing to their voters. On the other hand, large states that are currently competitive, such as Ohio or Florida, would stand to lose the most attention in the short run. And thus, putting together 270 electoral votes is likely to be a very slow and difficult process. Still, if agreed to, such a system would achieve the goal of making every citizen's vote count equally and provide incentives for parties to mobilize everywhere. Clearly, resource constraints would cause parties to concentrate larger efforts in more populated areas, but such efforts would still be more widespread than current undertakings. Such a plan will not see implementation in the foreseeable future, but as a long-term plan to bring about popular election of the president—something for which a majority of citizens consistently expresses support—this is a much more promising strategy than attempting to amend the U.S. Constitution.

The other strategy that could help in this regard is to increase the competitiveness of elections other than for the presidency. This would not make citizens feel as if their presidential vote mattered more, but it would create incentives for parties to mobilize more people and bring them into the electoral process in order to win these lower-level races. And we can see that this does matter. When we look at the top twelve states in terms of the increase of voter turnout (as seen in table 6-3, measured either by percentage of citizen population or percentage of voting-age population), four states on that list (South Dakota, Kentucky, Montana, and Utah) were not targeted at any time during the presidential campaign. And three of those states had competitive statewide elections—South Dakota and Kentucky at the senatorial level, and Montana at the gubernatorial level. Clearly, it is likely to be unusual for a state that is competitive at the state level to be non-competitive in the presidential race, since at the broadest level the forces that keep the parties competitive within the state are likely to affect both sets of elections. But as these three cases show, sometimes the idiosyncrasies of state campaigns can create a competitive race in what seems, from a presidential perspective, to be a noncompetitive situation. And when that happens, party mobilization is likely to occur.

More promising than additional state-level competition is increasing competitiveness in House races. Parties put strong mobilization efforts into competitive House districts, particularly given the close split we have in the House.[17] Even in states where the parties do not have strong mobilization efforts statewide, they will concentrate resources in competitive districts in an attempt to win those seats. Thus, even at the presidential level, maximizing the number of competitive House races would help by bringing more citizens into the process, often through face-to-face, grass-roots efforts. In this regard, of course, the problem is the continuing decline in the number of competitive districts.

There are many factors that contribute to the competitiveness or lack thereof of congressional districts, but the way in which district lines are drawn is clearly one of these factors.[18] And in the same ways in which campaigns can make use of more sophisticated technology to target voters, those drawing district lines can use computer technology to more effectively draw those lines to maximize their party's number of seats.[19] Some studies have argued that empirical evidence shows that redistricting contributes little or nothing to the lack of competitiveness of congressional elections and the resulting polarization in Congress as parties find that they have safe seats where they can advance more strident ideological positions.[20] But these studies miss the point, at least from the perspective of competitiveness. Drawing district lines may only change the number of districts that are competitive in any given election in a minimal way as so many other factors come into play. But over the long run, partisan gerrymandering does reduce the number of districts likely to be seen as "up for grabs." And those states that use outside organizations to control redistricting, most notably Iowa and Washington, tend to have more competitive elections than those states where the legislature controls redistricting.[21] Thus, efforts modeled after the Iowa system are more likely to create more competitive districts.[22]

TABLE 6-3: States with Largest Increases in Turnout, 2000–2004

	Increase Measured by Citizen VAP	Increase Measured by VAP
Arizona (PT)	11.3% (1)	7.6% (8)
Colorado (PT)	10.3% (2)	8.1% (6)
New Mexico (T)	10.0% (3)	9.6% (2)
Minnesota (T)	9.4% (4)	8.9% (3)
South Dakota (N)	9.1% (5)	8.4% (5)
Kentucky (N)	8.6% (6)	8.5% (4)
Arkansas (PT)	8.1% (7)	7.3% (9)
Utah (N)	7.6% (8)	6.5% (12)
Oregon (PT)	7.4% (9)	9.8% (1)
Montana (N)	7.3% (10)	7.7% (7)
Pennsylvania (T)	7.1% (11)	6.8% (10)
Ohio (T)	6.9% (12)	6.7% (11)

Percentages are the increases in turnout in 2004 compared to 2000 computed using both the voting age population (VAP) and population estimates excluding non-citizens. (See chapter 5 for a discussion of the dispute over which figures present a more accurate picture of turnout.) Number in parentheses is ranking of state in terms of size of increase by that particular method of determining turnout. The state turnout figures come from table A-5: Reported Voting and Registration for Total and Citizen Voting-Age Population by State as compiled by the U.S. Census Bureau, Current Population Report, released on-line on 26 May 2005 at http://www.census.gov/population/www/socdemo/voting/cps2004.html.

Fully Targeted (T) are those states that were on both parties' list the entire campaign; Partially Targeted (PT) were on the list of at least one of the parties for at least part of the campaign; Not Targeted (N) were not on either party's list at any time during the campaign.

Unfortunately, efforts in this regard are difficult to achieve. Parties tend to resist, as they prefer to keep the option of drawing lines in their favor when they control the legislature and, thus, have the power to change things. And the recent Supreme Court decision in the case of *League of United Latin American Citizens* v. *Perry*[23] only increases the potential difficulties in this area. In that case, the Court made clear that redistricting was permitted not only after the once-a-decade census, the standard practice, but multiple times in between, thus opening up the possibilities that parties who take control in the middle of a decade will immediately redistrict to their advantage or that parties will fine-tune the districts to make them even safer.[24]

Similarly, an attempt by California Governor Arnold Schwarzenegger to gain support for a citizen initiative that would have turned over redistricting to a nonpartisan commission was badly defeated in November 2005.[25] Unfortunately, in terms of the likelihood of success, this particular initiative was structured to have the first redistricting take place shortly after passage of the bill, allowing Democrats to claim it was simply a brazen attempt by the Republican Party to weaken the hold of the Democrats on the California congressional delegation. And anytime such a measure is easily portrayed as partisan, it is much harder to pass. A bill that would have shifted control, but not allowed for early redistricting, instead waiting for the 2010 census to kick in, might have been easier to sell to the public as a nonpartisan reform. And that, in turn, might have increased chances for passage.

Clearly, then, redistricting reform, which would lead to an increase in the number of competitive districts, could filter up to participation in the presidential election. But such reform is also quite difficult. It is most likely to win support when it can be portrayed as a nonpartisan, good-government reform. Delaying the implementation until after the next census, making it more difficult to predict which party might benefit—or how much partisan benefit is likely—can only help in that regard. Similarly, pushing for states to enact reform that would limit redistricting to once a decade would also improve the atmosphere for achieving broader redistricting reform.[26]

Reclaiming the Process: Increasing Voter Turnout

As we have seen, many Americans simply do not vote. Part of this is a result of their lack of interest in politics generally and their dissatisfaction with the political process. But some of it also has to do with the mechanics of voting. We make it very difficult, especially in comparison with other industrial democracies, for citizens to vote. Changing some of the rules in that regard would increase participation. Clearly, such reforms by themselves can only have limited effects, as we documented earlier. We have already been making it easier for people to vote, and in spite of that, turnout has been decreasing. But continuing to improve access to the polls can maximize turnout and make it easier for other changes to translate into higher participation.

The simplest reform, and one which those studying these issues agree would increase voter turnout, would be to allow Election Day Registration (EDR), something currently allowed in six states: Idaho, Maine, Minnesota, New Hampshire, Wisconsin, and Wyoming.[27] David Hill's examination of such reforms concluded that their impact is lagged. That is, it does not occur immediately, but builds up over time as voters learn to adjust to the new system.[28] Brians and Grofman, using longitudinal data, suggest that such a reform would increase voter turnout by about 7 percent.[29] And analysis of the 2004 election by Demos confirms this. They found that in "Battleground States" (those where the margin of victory was 5 percent or less), turnout was about 9 percent higher in EDR states than non-EDR states, while in safe states turnout was about 8 percent higher in EDR states.[30] Furthermore, 64 percent of the non-voting respondents to a survey done by the Medill School of Journalism reported that they would be more likely to vote should such a reform occur.[31] Clearly, such self-evaluation will overstate the likely impact of reforms, but it does show the extent to which non-voters see some of the rules we now have hindering their likelihood of going to the polls.

A second set of potential reforms would build on efforts to make balloting easier by allowing citizens to vote over an extended period time either in person or by mail. States vary dramatically in their rules regarding these matters, from Oregon, where all voting is done by mail, to fourteen states that do not allow any kind of early voting either in person or by mail. And of those states that allow early voting, some require an excuse, while others allow anyone to cast a ballot early.[32] Citizens do seem to like such options, and the percentage of citizens casting such early ballots increased from 14 percent in 2000 to 20 percent in 2004.[33] And in states where such an option is fairly easy, the percentage of voters taking advantage of this opportunity is quite large. Sixty-six percent of Washington voters, 32 percent of Arizona voters, 31 percent of California voters, and 29 percent of Colorado voters cast their ballots in this way.[34] Still, the increases brought about by such changes are likely to be modest. Karp and Banducci found that most of the citizens taking advantage of this option were voters likely to vote anyway, particularly in more visible elections such as a presidential campaign.[35] Similarly, a study of turnout in 2004 by the Center for the Study of the American Electorate found that these laws had a mixed impact, with the increases attributable to them to be minor, and clearly less than EDR, which had a clear, positive impact.[36] But studies done in the two states with the most extensive experience in these areas, Oregon and Washington, find clear evidence that they do increase turnout and that voters like the option.[37] Careful implementation of such laws can limit the likelihood of fraud and reduce the cost to election officials, actually increasing the integrity of the process.[38] On the other hand, these laws may increase the cost of campaigning, as the "last-minute blitz" at the end of the campaign needs to be spread out over a longer period of time,[39] and that raises more concerns about money and its role in the electoral process. Still, particularly if coupled with campaign finance reform to be discussed below, providing early voting and vote-by-mail options is likely to create an environment where citizens, finding it easier to vote, may be more willing to engage in the system if other changes can make that system more attractive to them.

Finally, we should note that some, particularly Arend Lijphart and Martin Wattenberg, argue that the best answer to the problem of low voter turnout would be to make voting compulsory.[40] But while making voting mandatory would clearly increase turnout, the likelihood of such a reform is limited at best. As Wattenberg reports, an ABC News poll in 2004 found that only 21 percent of the public supported such a law.[41] Fiorina's brief discussion of the issue notes that it is probably relatively easy to deal with the major objection raised to such a law, that is, people not wanting to be forced to vote for a candidate they did not like, by including a "none of the above" option or allowing submission of a blank ballot. But he also notes the major practical difficulty that would be harder to overcome: we vote so often in the United States for so many offices and issues that implementation would be remarkably burdensome for many people.[42] I am inclined to agree with this assessment, so I doubt that the work necessary to build support for such a measure would be worth the effort, as it seems unlikely that we are going to lessen the number of elections we have. Like eliminating the Electoral College, the barriers to compulsory voting make this a reform that should not be a focus of those wanting to reinvigorate our democracy. While smaller in potential impact, promoting easier access through Election Day registration or making it easier to vote early by mail are much more likely to be adopted and so make for a more sensible reform agenda.[43]

Reclaiming the Process: Campaign Finance Reform

As we have seen, one of the factors that contributes most strongly to the feelings of many that they do not count and that democracy is not working is the growing influence of money in our electoral process. The movement away from party-centered, labor-intensive election campaigns to candidate-centered, capital-intensive campaigns has, over time, raised the importance of money, leading to a growing sense that ordinary voters do not matter. The Bipartisan Campaign Reform Act, which began a new set of rules for campaign finance in 2004, was an attempt to deal with this concern. But while this did help in some ways (for example, a higher percentage of money came in smaller hard-money contributions, less in large contributions, and the ability of corporations and unions to provide direct funding of campaigns through soft money contributions was curtailed drastically), there is still much room for improvement.[44]

The most effective reform would be to move to a system of public finance, but there are difficulties both practical and theoretical with such an approach. On the practical side, the likelihood of passing such a reform in the foreseeable future is quite slim, as there is strong opposition to it both on theoretical grounds,[45] as something government should not be involved in, and from those who would stand to lose influence with such a change. Furthermore, even if public finance could be written into law, as long as the Supreme Court does not change its mind about the relationship between money and free speech in campaigns (something that does not seem likely), there will remain a role for private money in campaigns. And thus, laws and regulations steering private money in more positive directions will still be needed.

The best strategy for reform, then, would seem to be working to build support in the long run for a more comprehensive public finance system in order to limit the influence of private money as much as possible and to restore public confidence in the ability to make a difference in a campaign, while at the same time pressing for more immediate changes in the law to encourage the private finance system to shift in a positive direction. And to build support for public finance at the national level, the optimal strategy may be to work to change laws at the state level by promoting so-called "voter-owned election" reforms as a stepping-stone, showing through success how such changes can, in fact, make a difference.

These reforms work through a system of voluntary public financing. The exact details of the plans vary from state to state, but all work under the premise that providing sufficient public resources to candidates who meet reasonably constructed criteria can go a long way toward making elections more competitive, as well as cutting the ties between those who contribute to campaigns and the legislators whom they later influence.[46]

Two states, Maine and Arizona, have had significant success with these laws. According to a study by Kenneth Mayer, Timothy Werner, and Amanda Williams of the University of Wisconsin, "There is no question that public funding programs have increased the pool of candidates willing and able to run for state legislative office. The effect is most pronounced for challengers who were far more likely to accept public funding…[and] the reelection rate for incumbents in Maine and Arizona dropped significantly in 2002 and 2004 [after implementation of these laws]."[47]

The authors of this study also note the importance of adequate funding for these laws, as states attempting to implement them without such funding have not proven as successful. These studies, and others, are available from both the Wisconsin Campaign Finance Project and the Institute on Money in State Politics.[48] Suffice it to say that there is evidence that such laws can make a difference. And as recently as December 2005, Connecticut became the first state to pass legislation at the state level establishing a system of voter-owned elections.[49] In all previous cases, voter initiative or referendum was the route by which these laws were passed. Efforts are under way in many states, most visibly California, to build on this success and spread reform. According to Public Campaign, there are activists in thirty states working for such legislation.[50] And Representatives John Tierney (D-MA) and Raul Grijalva (D-AZ) have introduced legislation to create a system of public finance for House elections. But state-level efforts seem a more promising way to approach this issue until more citizens and political leaders have had experience with these elections. Success in a large state such as California would seem particularly important in building support at the national level.

In the meantime, there are a number of reforms that could build upon BCRA and improve the finance system. First, one of the perverse effects of BCRA, as we have seen, was to make it less likely for candidates for president to accept public funds, particularly in the nomination stage. Steps should be taken to make it more likely that candidates will accept those public funds. To do so, the match of public to private funds should be increased, and the state-by-state limits on spending that come with taking the private funds should either be eliminated, leaving only an overall limit which should also be increased, or refigured to take into account the timing of the primaries and caucuses, allowing more spending in earlier states than is currently allowed when a formula relying only on the size of the state is used. And some kind of provision needs to be added to allow candidates facing opponents who opt out of public funding in order to be able to spend more to increase their spending as well. The specific details of such reforms are less important than the general principles, but as a starting point the recommendations of the Campaign Finance Institute's Task Force on Financing Presidential Elections are very reasonable. They recommend a three-to-one match of the first $100 and an earlier start date for the disbursement of funds to increase the impact of small donations in the crucial early stages of the campaign, and an increase in the overall spending limits to the same level as the general election limit ($75 million in 2004, indexed to inflation in future years), paying for the increased costs by increasing the tax check-off to $5.[51] And legislation introduced in the Senate by Russ Feingold (D-WI) and in the House by Christopher Shays (R-CT) and Marty Meehan (D-MA), three of the four lead authors of BCRA,[52] was endorsed by CFI as consistent with its approach.[53]

Other steps could also be taken to improve the climate of public finance. Disclosure for contributions to 527 organizations could be improved, as could disclosure to other charitable groups that engage in political spending, even if it is "bipartisan." But as a working paper of the Campaign Finance Institute argued, changes in disclosure for 527 groups needs to be done in the context of more comprehensive reform that also targets the other types of groups that organizations use to fund politics. In a study of twelve different organizations, CFI found that many groups used multiple avenues to funnel money into the political system including 527s, PACs, and a variety of 501 groups. Thus, changes in disclosure or regulations tightening what 527s can do is likely to shift money into 501(c) groups unless rules are also implemented that will allow fuller disclosure and control of activities by those groups.[54] The key here is to make the system as transparent as possible. If private money is going to play a role—and it will—citizens need to know who is providing the funds. Transparency makes vibrant democracy more possible. It will not, as we have seen, eliminate the influence of money. But it can minimize that influence by providing awareness and by making it easier for those who rely on organizing citizens rather than money to have a visible target around which to build public awareness and mobilization.

Finally, if private money is going to enter the system and not go to candidates, it is better to funnel that money through political parties than through interest groups, as the parties are more directly accountable and—in spite of growing polarization between the parties—have more incentive to promote the kind of centrist policies that citizens may prefer, in contrast to groups who have much less incentive to compromise.[55] Eliminating soft money and the extremely large, often direct corporate or union contributions that it involved, was important to restoring the integrity of the system. And I would not suggest going back to that system. But raising the level of hard-money contributions that can be given to parties in a year above the current $95,000 would encourage more money to flow through the parties. Clearly, it is important not to let that level rise too much, but doubling it, in a campaign environment where the parties need hundreds of millions of dollars to run national campaigns, would funnel more funds into parties and away from PACs, 527s, and 501(c)s. And that is a more accountable source. Voters can more easily blame (and, therefore, hold accountable) candidates for what their party is doing than they can blame independent groups. And that is an important step if citizens are to feel as if they, not those with money, can exercise democratic control.

Reclaiming the Process: What Parties, Media, and Citizens Can Do

Aside from the kinds of systemic reforms discussed above, there are other things that various actors in the electoral process can do that would help increase the democratic efficacy of our system. As we have seen, it is crucial that citizens feel connected with that system and that they matter. And, perhaps, the key actors in creating such connections are the political parties. Rebuilding (or building, as the case may be) the political parties as more grass-roots-oriented organizations can go a long way toward rebuilding democratic connections for citizens. The development of new technologies can help in this regard, but there are also forces that can hinder positive changes. Parties have learned that they can use computer technology and the World Wide Web as an effective organizing tool. But the most effective uses from a democratic perspective are those that use the web to build local organizations through things such as "meet-ups," or local house parties, and other face-to-face events. Short-term electoral forces often provide incentive to focus such activity exclusively in competitive districts or states,[56] but we are most likely to improve citizen feelings about the system if such efforts are undertaken everywhere, regardless of the competitiveness of a particular geographic location. Parties do have a long-term interest in building support everywhere, which is why they—not candidates or interest groups—are best suited for such an emphasis. And so we should try to encourage the parties to make such efforts. Howard Dean, the 2004 candidate who, more than any other candidate, saw the organizing potential of the Internet, has begun to implement a "fifty-state policy" as chair of the Democratic National Committee. This policy has met with some resistance from the "Washington insiders" who would prefer the DNC concentrate its resources on those races most likely to be essential in recapturing control of Congress, but Dean, with support from state party chairs, has continued to promote this broader, less targeted strategy.[57] And that, from a long-term democratic perspective, is a good thing. The healthiest course for our democracy would be for both parties to adopt strategies designed to organize and build the parties in every state.

In a similar fashion, new web technologies can continue to be exploited to promote more positive democratic activities. One welcome development in campaign finance in the last election was the growth in the percentage of funds that came from small donors. And that, clearly, was a function of the exploitation and use of web technology. A study of small donors and on-line giving by the Institute for Politics, Democracy and the Internet at George Washington University concluded that "the Internet has helped level the playing field between large donors and small donors…[by helping] small, less experienced donors broaden their reach and, hence their influence with others."[58] And the report found that this fundraising from small donors was tied to other grass-roots organizing activities, as a quarter of all donors reported attending a political house party, and that this method of giving was particularly attractive to younger citizens, with more than 80 percent of those age 18 to 34 who gave to campaigns giving on-line.[59] Furthermore, it is clear that parties and candidates have learned this and are now incorporating such activities into their planning and organizing.[60] And this is another positive development. The one risk here is that the activists attracted to such activity will be polarizing, and early studies of those who get involved on-line by blogging and other activities do find, not surprisingly, that those who are involved in these activities are not a representative cross-section of the population.[61] However, in terms of partisanship and attitudes, what we know about these people is not as threatening to democratic discourse as we might think. While the issue agenda of bloggers may differ from that of the general public, they do not seem to be much more partisan as an audience. In fact, many more are unaffiliated with either party than is typical of the general public, and this likely reflects the greater distrust they have of our political system.[62] Furthermore, those who blog prefer to get their news from balanced, as opposed to partisan, sources.[63] Still, it is also clear that the web makes it much easier for citizens to get messages that simply reinforce their partisan predispositions and have the effect of creating greater polarization.[64] And the broader figures cited by the Davis and Lenhart and Fox studies may underestimate this polarizing influence, as they do not measure the actual content of what is seen on the web, but rather measure the attitudes of the people who are using it. And anyone who has spent time reading through the postings at various political sites knows how partisan and divisive they can be. So it becomes important to try to encourage use of the web that promotes healthier, democratic deliberation. Here some of the suggestions that Davis makes seem appropriate.[65]

After examining current uses and users of the web, Davis suggests that we try to create public spaces on the web, spaces where citizens can "express themselves as members of a polity and find common ground and even consensus for political action. It [would be] a sphere of respect and appreciation for contrasting views. But it [would not be] limited to a mechanism for expression. It [would be] a vehicle for public deliberation and problem solving."[66] As Davis argues, such public spaces can promote a sense of community. Participants must feel that they have a stake in these deliberations, and that can be aided by a commitment by public officials to participate in, or at least monitor, these forums. These spaces would require a nonpartisan moderator to shape and guide discussion and keep the space comfortable for participants, drawing in as many people as possible. This would allow discussion to move beyond the "mere expression" of opinion to more substantive public deliberation and allow learning to occur.[67] And it would empower citizens by allowing them to help set the public agenda and contribute to the decisions that public officials make.[68] Such sites could be administered by educational institutions, nonpartisan groups (either existing or newly established), or current commercial entities as part of a commitment to public good, so long as these commercial entities did not exercise control over the sites, thus insuring that the space is truly public and participants are citizens, not customers.[69]

The Internet could clearly serve this purpose. It "possesses the potential to serve as such a mechanism. The creation of such electronic public space is achievable if current knowledge about the requirements for public deliberation is applied, and if interests seeking to use public space for narrow policy ends are kept in check."[70] And there are efforts under way to create such public spaces. Project Vote Smart, for example, is an organization that tries to provide information to allow citizens to check on the records and platforms of candidates and elected officials at the local, state, and national levels.[71] And Minnesota E-Democracy has created, since 1994, such a public space for deliberation focused on elections in Minnesota, an effort it hopes to spread to other locations.[72]

Public forums such as these could reconnect citizens with the democratic process and, in doing so, strengthen the electoral process as well. They could exist alongside and in between our elections, drawing citizens into the process in more productive ways. But for them to work, we need "a willingness on the part of all concerned to engage in innovativeness."[73]

But changing citizen attitudes so that we will become more involved will not be easy, and this leads to the ways in which two other actors in the political process might evolve in ways that would help promote a more active, democratic process: the media and our educational system.

In terms of media, the major challenge is the growing politicization of the news audience, with Republicans and Democrats relying on and trusting different news organizations.[74] The starkest example of this found by the Pew Research Center was that Fox News was the most trusted source for Republicans, the least trusted for Democrats.[75] But the most troubling pattern is the overall decline in trust in news sources.[76] Media outlets of all types need to work to rebuild their credibility. An audience that is too cynical of what it reads or hears and too divided over which source it might trust, is less well equipped to engage in public dialogue. Two news sources currently appear on the list of the six most believable news sources for Republicans, Democrats, and Independents: CNN and C-SPAN. CNN is the most-believed source among Democrats (45 percent believe all or most of what they report), and ranks second among Independents (28 percent) and Republicans (26 percent), while C-SPAN ranks third among both Democrats (36 percent) and Independents (26 percent) and fifth among Republicans (22 percent).[77] Clearly, these sources need to work to maintain that broad credibility, and other media sources need to strive to achieve that as well.

On a more promising note, Pew did find, however, that after years of decline, newspapers are now using their on-line editions to stem readership loss, and that as the news audience for the Internet matures, it has begun to develop in a way where the web content of the news is seen as a good place for headlines and quick information, but with a recognition of the need to go elsewhere for more in-depth news.[78] And this does provide some hope that more depth-oriented, nonpartisan websites can become more important sources for citizens, improving the likelihood that citizens will gather the kinds of information that would be most helpful to them in becoming more active citizens.

This leaves us with the final hope for change, improved civic education. Whenever I discuss issues of elections, democracy, and participation with my students, the need for better civic education is a recurring theme in student suggestions and concerns.[79] And we know that better civic education does improve student knowledge about government and politics.[80] Even something as simple as actually teaching students how to use voting machines can lead to increased voter turnout.[81] My students always recognize, particularly when they trade stories about the relative quality of their high school civic education, that if schools did a better job in this regard, the pool of citizens able to participate in civic life would increase. Furthermore, today's youth are not, according to research done by the Pew Research Center, as disengaged as we often think. In fact, "many are engaged in volunteer activities and community problem-solving, and even more voice their opinions on public issues through the internet and more conventional media...with [about 40 percent saying] they had done some type of volunteer work in the past year."[82] Civic education that improves student understanding of the political process and encourages student involvement in local civic affairs can help to build relationships to the community that can translate into participation in politics at the national level.[83]

For the past forty years, the trends have been moving in a direction that removes the public from the democratic process. We have been voting less, caring less, and leaving our governance to those with money and passion, the two factors that seem to have kept people involved and feeling important. But a democracy whose elections engage few citizens and in which those with money seem to matter too much is not a healthy democracy. These trends will not be easy to reverse, but the Internet and other technologies provide tools that can help us in the process. And the election of 2004 provided a glimpse of some of that potential, though it also provided evidence of the difficulties of converting this new technology into a tool for democracy. With proper reforms and changes in practices and attitudes, we can reclaim our democracy.

The struggle for democracy is never an easy one,[84] but it is always worthwhile. And the Internet provides the best tool ever invented (or at least since the invention of movable type!) for empowering people. Better rules and regulations, reforms along the lines outlined in this chapter, can help. But in the end it is up to us, the people, to decide that our democracy is worth fighting for and work to establish procedures that will enhance our ability to participate. We may not agree on what we want to do—rising differences over goals can make democracy seem more threatening and dangerous to some—and issues of process rarely seem compelling to people. But without developing a system where people feel that they are heard and that they matter, without a system where the public participates and works to influence the outcomes of elections, and without a system where political leaders feel a need to listen to constituents, then what we want becomes irrelevant, and battles over outcomes will take place without concern for the public. We need to tap into the spirit of community and commitment to a public life that we saw when people lined up to donate blood after the attacks of 9/11. We need to build the capacity of our democracy to respond to the desires of the people. For the past forty years we have been losing control. We need to take it back.

Notes

1 Some of the better accounts and analyses of the 2004 elections are Nelson, Michael, ed., *The Elections of 2004* (Washington, DC: CQ Press, 2005); Ceaser, James, and Busch, Andrew, *Red Over Blue* (Lanham, MD: Rowman & Littlefield, 2005); Crotty, William, *A Defining Moment* (Armonk, NY: M.E. Sharpe, 2005); Magleby, David; Monson, Quin; and Patterson, Kelly, eds., *Dancing Without Partners* (Lanham, MD: Rowman & Littlefield, 2006); and Abramson, Paul; Aldrich, John; and Rohde, David, *Change and Continuity in the 2004 Elections* (Washington, DC: CQ Press, 2006).

2 For the seminal discussion of rally effects, see Mueller, John, *War, Presidents and Public Opinion* (New York: John Wiley and Sons, 1973). Also see Brace, Paul, and Hinckley, Barbara, *Follow the Leader* (New York: Basic Books, 1992); and Kernell, Samuel, *Going Public*, 3rd ed. (Washington, DC: CQ Press, 1997).

3 See Green, Donald, and Gerber, Alan, *Get Out the Vote* (Washington, DC: Brookings Institution, 2004). In discussing the research done for the study that resulted in the book *Dancing Without Partners*, David Magleby noted how many of the representatives of parties and interest groups interviewed for that project mentioned the lessons of the Green and Gerber book in noting why they undertook such extensive grass-roots campaigns. These comments were made at a conference devoted to that study and its implications at the National Press Club in Washington, DC, on February 7, 2005.

4 See Magleby et al., *Dancing Without Partners*. The case-study chapters in the book provide strong evidence of the efforts at mobilization by both parties and independent groups. Most of the Republican activity was funneled through the party or the Bush-Cheney campaign, though

there was some additional group effort. On the Democratic side, the actions of groups were much more extensive.

5 Bergan, Daniel; Gerber, Alan; Green, Donald; and Panagopoulos, Costas, "Grassroots Mobilization and Voter Turnout in 2004," *Public Opinion Quarterly* 69 (2005): Special Issue, no. 5, 760–77.

6 Green, Donald; Palmquist, Bradley; and Schickler, Eric, *Partisan Hearts and Minds* (New Haven, CT: Yale University Press, 2002), ch. 8. The quotation appears on p. 225.

7 For an argument that these longer-term forces will lead to the growth of a natural Democratic majority, see Judas, John, and Teixeria, Rudy, *The Emerging Democratic Majority* (New York: Scribner, 2004). For an alternative perspective, see Hamburger, Tom, and Wallsten, Peter, *One Party Country* (New York: Wiley, 2006).

8 Bergan et al., "Grassroots Mobilization and Voter Turnout in 2004," 776.

9 See the Moveon.org website at www.moveon.org/about.html.

10 See the Democracy for America website at www.democracyforamerica.com/aboutdfa.php.

11 See Nagourney, Adam, "Democrats Propose Moving Up Nevada in Presidential Caucuses," *The New York Times*, 23 July 2006, A1.

12 See Clymer, Adam, "The 2000 Campaign: The Primaries; G.O.P. Panel Votes to Revise Primary System," *The New York Times,* 3 May 2000, A1.

13 See Clymer, Adam, "The 2000 Campaign: The Process; A G.O.P. Overhaul of Primary Season Is Killed by Bush," *The New York Times*, 29 July 2000, A1.

14 Patterson is quoted on this point in Clymer, Adam, "The 2000 Campaign: The Primaries; G.O.P. Panel Votes to Revise Primary System," *The New York Times*, 13 May 2000, A12.

15 A detailed description of the plan can be found in Koza, John, et al., *Every Vote Equal* (Los Altos, CA: National Popular Vote Press, 2006). The book can be viewed or downloaded at no charge at http://www.every-vote-equal.com/index.html.

16 The National Popular Vote website at http://www.nationalpopularvote.com/npv/ tracks news about this effort. The particular actions referred to were some of the headlines in the "recent news" summary on July 27, 2006.

17 See the case studies of congressional districts in Magleby et al., *Dancing Without Partners*, chs. 14–22.

18 For an overview of these issues see Jacobson, Gary, *The Politics of Congressional Elections*, 6th ed. (New York: Pearson Longman, 2004), esp. ch. 2; and Herrnson, Paul, *Congressional Elections*, 4th ed. (Washington, DC: CQ Press, 2004), particularly ch. 1.

19 See Butler, David, and Cain, Bruce, *Congressional Redistricting* (New York: Macmillan, 1992).

20 See, for example, Ono, Keiko, "Electoral Origins of Partisan Polarization in Congress: Debunking the Myth," *Extensions, A Journal of the Carl Albert Congressional Research and Studies Center* (Fall 2005): 15–19, 25.

21 Abramowitz, Alan, *Voice of the People* (Boston: McGraw-Hill, 2004), 251–52.

22 In Iowa, the state where I reside, the job of drawing district lines falls to the nonpartisan Legislative Services Bureau (LSB), whose mandate is to draw districts with close to equal populations without dividing any county into two districts. The state legislature then must approve of the plan with an up-or-down vote. No amendments are allowed, and the governor must sign off on it as well. If it is not approved, the LSB draws up a second plan. If that sec-

ond plan is not approved, then the legislature must draw the lines themselves. Given the political culture of Iowa, turning down that second plan is seen as politically risky. After the census of 2000, the LSB drew up a map that created four competitive districts out of five seats. As it turned out, the incumbents were victorious in all of those races, but that did not mean that the parties did not target and mobilize in all of those campaigns. See Redlawsk, David, and Sanders, Arthur, "The Iowa Senate and 1st, 2nd, 3rd, and 4th Congressional District Races," in Magleby, David, and Monson, Quin, eds., *The Last Hurrah* (Provo, UT: The Center for the Study of Elections and Democracy, 2003), ch. 3; and Redlawsk, David, and Sanders, Arthur, "The 2002 Iowa House and Senate Elections: The More Things Change…" *PS* 36 (July 2003): 406, (abstract) and at www.apsanet.org/PS/july03/redlawsk.pdf (article).

23 Nos. 05-204, 05-254, 05-276 and 05-439, 399 F. Supp. 2d 756, available at http://supct.law.cornell.edu/supct/html/05-204.ZS.html.

24 See Blumenthal, Ralph, and Zernike, Kate, "Day of Joy Dawns for Republicans, Proud Owners of Texas Districting Map," *The New York Times*, 29 June 2006, A22.

25 See Broder, John, "The 2005 Elections: California; Not on Ballot, Schwarzenegger Is Still Rebuked," *The New York Times*, 10 November 2005, A1.

26 The League of Women Voters is one "good-government" group that has taken on the cause of redistricting reform, but thus far they have had very little success. See their discussion of the issue and their efforts at http://www.lwv.org/AM/Template.cfm?Section=Redistricting.

27 For an overview in support of this reform, see the Election Day Registration area of Demos at www.demos-usa.org/page52.cfm.

28 Hill, David, *American Voter Turnout* (Boulder, CO: Westview Press, 2006), 53–55.

29 Brians, Craig, and Grofman, Bernard, "Election Day Registration's Effect on U.S. Voter Turnout," *Social Science Quarterly* 82 (2001): 170–83.

30 See "High 2004 Turnout for States with Election Day Registration," at www.demos.org/page18.cfm. The EDR battleground states had turnout of 75.7 percent, while non-EDR battleground states had turnout of 66.8 percent. In safe states it was 66.9 percent compared to 58.5 percent.

31 See the EDR project of Demos.

32 For a detailed list of state laws on absentee and early voting, see http://electionline.org/Default.aspx?tabid=474. Also see Holder, Kelly, "Voting and Registration in the Election of November 2004," *USCensusBureau*, Report issued March 2006. The PDF file with the report can be downloaded at http://www.census.gov/population /www/socdemo/voting.html.

33 National Annenberg Election Survey, "Early Voting Reaches Record Levels in 2004, National Annenberg Election Survey Shows," Press Release, 24 March 2005. The press release and other information about early voting can be found at the Early Voting page of Reformelections.org, at http://reformelections.org/feature.asp?menuid={88D32B4338764B06A94125A33211CBE5}.

34 Holder, Kelly, "Voting and Registration in the Election of November 2004," 11.

35 Karp, Jeffrey, and Banducci, Susan, "Going Postal: How All-Mail Elections Influence Turnout," *Political Behavior* 22 (2000): 223–39.

36 See Gans, Curtis, "Turnout Exceeds Optimistic Predictions. More Than 122 Million Vote. Highest Turnout in 38 Years." The report can be downloaded at the at the Early Voting page of Reformelections.org at http://reformelections.org/feature.asp?menuid={88D32B43-3876-

4B06-A941-25A33211CBE5}. It is also worth noting that previous reports by this group had been critical of these reforms. See, for example, Gans, Curtis, "Making It Easier Doesn't Work," also available for download at the Voting Page of Reformelection.org. The finding of no impact earlier, but some in 2004, fits Hill's argument that there is a lag in the time it takes for these laws to have an impact.

37 See Southwell, Priscella, "Five Years Later: A Re-Assessment of Oregon's Vote by Mail Electoral Process," and the Washington State Association of County Auditors, "Mail Voting in the Stadium Election," 28 July 1997, both available for download at the website of the Oregon Secretary of State at http://www.sos.state.or.us/executive/policy-initiatives/vbm/exec vbm.htm.

38 See Gronke, Paul, *Ballot Integrity and Voting by Mail: The Oregon Experience*, A Report for the Commission on Federal Election Reform, also available for download at the website of the Oregon Secretary of State.

39 See "Stamp of Approval?" *The Economist*, 16 March 2006, viewed at www.economist.com /World/na/displayStory.cfm?story_id=5636390.

40 See Lijphart, Arend, "Compulsory Voting Is the Best Way to Keep Democracy Strong," *Chronicle of Higher Education*, 18 October 1996, B: 3–4 and Wattenberg, Martin, *Is Voting for Young People* (New York: Pearson Longman, 2007), esp. ch. 7.

41 Wattenberg, *Is Voting for Young People*, 170, table 7-2.

42 Fiorina, Morris, *Culture War? The Myth of a Polarized America*, 2nd ed. (New York: Pearson Longman, 2006), 219–22.

43 Increasing voting rights for convicted felons, discussed in chapter 5, is also a reform worth pursuing.

44 For the best summary of the impact of BCRA, see Malbin, Michael, ed., *The Election After Reform* (Lanham, MD: Rowman & Littlefield, 2006); and Magleby et al., *Dancing Without Partners*.

45 See the articles opposing campaign finance reform at the Cato Institute's website at http://www.cato.org/research/crg/finance.html.

46 For the most comprehensive look at these laws and their history and impact, go to the website of Public Campaign, a non-profit organization dedicated to establishing voter-owned elections across the nation, http://www.publicampaign.org/clean123.

47 Mayer, Kenneth; Werner, Timothy; and Williams, Amanda, "Do Public Funding Programs Enhance Electoral Competition?" Updated version, March 2005, 6. Available at the website of the Wisconsin Campaign Finance Project at http://campfin.polisci.wisc.edu/.

48 The Institute on Money in State Politics can be found at http://www.followthemoney.org/. Among the studies is one by Megan Moore, "Clean Elections: Arizona 2004." Similarly, in addition to the Mayer, Werner, and Williams study cited in note 47 above, there are a number of other studies at this website. And both of these organizations provide data on state-level campaign finance.

49 The law takes effect for the 2008 election. See Pazniakos, Mark, and Keating, Christopher, "Senate Passes Reform Package," *The Hartford Courant*, 1 December 2005, A1; and Pazniakos, Mark, "Campaign Finance Reform Becomes Law," *The Hartford Courant*, 8 December 2005, B8. The law was strengthened in May 2006 by adding some ethics provisions that had been left out of the original bill. See Keating, Christopher, and Hamilton, Elizabeth, "A Deal

at Last," *The Hartford Courant*, 4 May 2006, A1.

50 See http://www.publiccampaign.org/clean123.

51 See *So the Voters May Choose*, available for download at the Campaign Finance Institute's website at http://www.cfinst.org/presidential/report2/index.html.

52 The absence of the fourth, Senator John McCain (R-AZ), was striking, and clear evidence of the difficulty facing such legislation.

53 Campaign Finance Institute, Press Release, "New Presidential Public Financing Bill: A First Step for Empowering the Voters," 28 July 2006. Available at http://www.cfinst.org/pr/072806.html.

54 Weissman, Stephen, and Ryan, Kara, "Non-Profit Interest Groups' Election Activities and Federal Campaign Finance Policy" (Washington, DC: The Campaign Finance Institute, July 2006). The summary of the report and a link to download the report can be found at http://www.cfinst.org/pr/071906.html.

55 In fact, as we have seen, the growing influence of groups within the parties has contributed to the increase in polarization.

56 Which reinforces the proposals above designed to increase the number of competitive districts.

57 Dean announced this strategy when campaigning for the position of DNC chair. See Nagourney, Adam, "Democrats Hear from 8 Who Want to Lead Party," *The New York Times*, 12 December 2004, 1:44. The strategy itself can be seen at the DNC's website at http://www.democrats.org/a/party/a_50_state_strategy/. For the battle within the party over this strategy, see Nagourney, Adam, "Dean and Party Leaders in a Money Dispute," *The New York Times*, 11 May 2006, A31; and Gilgoff, Dan, "Dean's List," *U.S. News and World Report*, 24 July 2006, available at http://www.usnews.com/usnews/news/articles/060716/24dems.htm. Dean's defense of the policy can be seen at http://www.democrats.org/a/2006/06/50-state_strate_1.php. And for an op-ed piece defending Dean's strategy as good for the party, see Galvin, Daniel, "How to Grow a Democratic Majority," *The New York Times*, 3 June 2006, A13.

58 The Institute for Politics, Democracy and the Internet, *Small Donors and Online Giving* (Washington, DC: The George Washington University Graduate School of Political Management, 2005), 2.

59 Ibid.

60 Nagourney, Adam, "Internet Injects Sweeping Change into U.S. Politics," *The New York Times*, 2 April 2006, 1:1.

61 Davis, Richard, *Politics Online* (New York: Routledge, 2005); and Lenhart, Amanda, and Fox, Susannah, *Bloggers* (Washington, DC: The Pew Internet and American Life Project), 19 July 2006, available at http://www.pewinternet.org/.

62 Davis, *Politics Online*, 107–17.

63 Lenhart and Fox, *Bloggers*, 5.

64 Sunstein, Cass, *republic.com* (Princeton, NJ: Princeton University Press, 2001).

65 The discussion that follows, in addition to the specific citations below, draws on the general discussion by Davis in ch. 6 of *Politics Online*, particularly 126–38.

66 Davis, *Politics Online*, 126.

67 In addition to Davis, see Mathews, David, *Politics for People: Finding a Responsible Voice*

(Urbana: University of Illinois Press, 1994).

68 Some of the strongest arguments in favor of a stronger, more active, participatory democracy can be found in the work of Benjamin Barber. See, for example, *Strong Democracy: Participatory Democracy for a New Age* (Berkeley: University of California Press, 2004); *A Place for Us: How to Make Society Civil and Democracy Strong* (New York: Hill and Wang, 1998); and "Globalizing Democracy," *The American Prospect*, 11 September 2000, on-line at http://www.prospect.org/print-friendly/print/V11/20/barber-b.html.

69 Davis, *Politics Online*, 128.

70 Ibid., 135.

71 Go to http://www.vote-smart.org/index.htm. I serve on the advisory board, which helps identify key votes in state legislatures (in my case in Iowa) for inclusion in the database, so I can attest to the care they take to be fair and nonpartisan in choosing which issues to examine.

72 See their website at http://www.e-democracy.org/. They also have established forums to discuss election issues in the United Kingdom.

73 Davis, *Politics Online*, 137.

74 See the report by the Pew Research Center for the People and the Press, *Online News Audience Larger, More Diverse. News Audience Increasingly Politicized*, 8 June 2004. The report can be downloaded at http://people-press.org/reports/display.php3?ReportID=215.

75 Ibid., 44.

76 Ibid., 40–44.

77 The chart with these figures can be found in *Online News Audience Larger, More Diverse*, 44.

78 See the report by the Pew Research Center for the People and the Press, *Maturing Internet News Audience—Broader Than Deep; Online Papers Modestly Boost Newspaper Readership*, 30 July 2006. The report can be downloaded at http://people-press.org/reports/display.php3?ReportID=282.

79 Martin Wattenberg reports a similar experience in *Is Voting for Young People*, 162.

80 Niemi, Richard, and Junn, Jane, *Civic Education: What Makes Students Learn* (New Haven, CT: Yale University Press, 1998).

81 Addonizio, Elizabeth, "Practice Makes Perfect: How Hands-On Familiarity with the Voting Process Increases Voter Turnout among 18 Year-Olds," Paper Presented at the Annual Meeting of the American Political Science Association, Chicago, IL, 2–5 September 2004.

82 Keeter, Scott, "Politics and the 'DotNet' Generation," Pew Research Center, 30 May 2006. Found at http://pewresearch.org/obdeck/?ObDeckID=27. For a fuller report see Zukin, Cliff, et al. *A New Engagement? Political Participation, Civic Life, and the Changing American Citizen* (New York: Oxford University Press, 2006).

83 Macedo, Stephen, et al., *Democracy at Risk* (Washington, DC: Brookings Institution Press, 2005), also recommends working to build local-level participation and local politics as a way to enhance political efficacy and, thus, to build a national democratic community more generally. They also recommend improved civic education.

84 For a wonderful history of the struggle for democracy in nineteenth-century America, one that reminds us that we have faced these struggles before and have overcome, at least in part, the challenges that we have faced, see Wilenz, Sean, *The Rise of American Democracy: Jefferson to Lincoln* (New York: W.W. Norton, 2005).

BIBLIOGRAPHY

Abramowitz, Alan, *Voice of the People: Elections and Voting in the United States* (Boston: McGraw-Hill, 2004).

Abramowitz, Alan, and Stone, Walter, *Nomination Politics: Party Activists and Presidential Choice* (New York: Praeger, 1984).

Abramson, Jill, "Campaign Finance: Audit Faults Clinton and Dole Ads," *The New York Times*, 11 December 1998, A1, A24.

Abramson, Paul, *Political Attitudes in America* (San Francisco: W.H. Freeman, 1983).

Abramson, Paul; Aldrich, John; and Rohde, David, *Change and Continuity in the 2004 Elections* (Washington, DC: CQ Press, 2006).

Addonizio, Elizabeth, "Practice Makes Perfect: How Hands-On Familiarity with the Voting Process Increases Voter Turnout among 18 Year-Olds," a Paper Presented at the Annual Meeting of the American Political Science Association, Chicago, IL, 2–5 September 2004.

Alexander, Herbert, *Financing Politics: Money, Elections and Political Reform* (Washington, DC: Congressional Quarterly, 1984).

Anderson, Nick, "Democrats Spend $3.5 Million on N.H. Primary Ad Blitz," *The Los Angeles Times*, 27 January 2004, accessed at http://www.latimes.com/news/nation/la-naads27jan 27,1,5037374.story?coll=la-headlines-nation.

Ansolabehere, Stephen, and Konisky, David, "The Introduction of Voter Registration and Its Effect on Turnout," *Political Analysis* 14 (2006): 83–100.

Atkeson, Lonna, "Divisive Primaries and General Election Outcomes: Another Look at Presidential Campaigns," *American Journal of Political Science* 42 (1998): 256–71.

___,"From the Primaries to the General Election: Does a Divisive Nomination Race Affect a Candidate's Fortunes in the Fall?," in Mayer, William, ed., *In Pursuit of the White House 2000* (New York: Chatham House, 2000), 285–312.

Barber, Benjamin, "Globalizing Democracy," *The American Prospect*, 11 September 2000.

___, *A Place for Us: How to Make Society Civil and Democracy Strong* (New York: Hill and Wang, 1998).

___, *Strong Democracy: Participatory Democracy for a New Age* (Berkeley: University of California Press, 2004).

Bartels, Larry, *Presidential Primaries and the Dynamics of Public Choice* (Princeton, NJ: Princeton University Press, 1988).

Beaumont, Thomas, "9 Potential Presidential Candidates Plan Trips," *Des Moines Register*, 1 August 2006, accessed at http://desmoinesregister.com/apps/pbcs.dll/article?AID=/2006 0801/NEWS09/608010381/1056.

Bergan, Daniel; Gerber, Alan; Green, Donald; and Panagopoulos, Costas, "Grassroots Mobilization and Voter Turnout in 2004," *Public Opinion Quarterly* 69 (Special Issue 2005, Number 5): 760–77.

Berns, Walter, ed., *After the People Vote: A Guide to the Electoral College* (Washington, DC: American Enterprise Institute, 1992).

Bernstein, Jonathan, "The *New* New Presidential Elite," in Mayer, William, ed., *In Pursuit of the White House 2000* (New York: Chatham House, 2000).

Bernstein, Robert, "Divisive Primaries Do Hurt: U.S. Senate Races, 1956–1972," *American Political Science Review* 71 (1977): 540–45.

Berry, Jeffrey, *The New Liberalism* (Washington, DC: Brookings Institution Press, 1999).

Bibby, John, "Party Organizations, 1946–1996," in Shafer, Byron, ed., *Partisan Approaches to Postwar American Politics* (New York: Chatham House, 1998), 142–85.

___, *Politics, Parties, and Elections in America*, 5th ed. (Belmont, CA: Wadsworth/Thomas Learning, 2003).

Blumenthal, Ralph, and Zernike, Kate, "Day of Joy Dawns for Republicans, Proud Owners of Texas Districting Map," *The New York Times*, 29 June 2006, A22.

Brace, Paul, and Hinckley, Barbara, *Follow the Leader* (New York: Basic Books, 1992).

Brennan Center for Justice, "2000 Presidential Race First in Modern History Where Political Parties Spend More on TV Ads Than Candidates, " Press Release, New York, 11 December 2000.

Brereton, Charles, *First in the Nation: New Hampshire and the Premier Presidential Primary* (Portsmouth, NH: Peter Randall, 1987).

Brians, Craig, and Grofman, Bernard, "Election Day Registrations' Effect on U.S. Voter Turnout," *Social Science Quarterly* 82 (2001): 170–83.

___, "When Election Barriers Fall," *Public Choice* 99 (1999): 161–76.

Broder, John, "The 2005 Elections: California; Not on Ballot, Schwarzenegger Is Still Rebuked," *The New York Times*, 10 November 2005, A1.

Brody, Richard, "The Puzzle of Political Participation in America," in King, Anthony, ed., *The New American Political System* (Washington, DC: The American Enterprise Institute, 1978).

Buell, Emmett, Jr., "The Changing Face of the New Hampshire Primary," in Mayer, William, ed., *In Pursuit of the White House 2000* (New York: Chatham House, 2000), 87–144.

Buhr, Tami, "What Voters Know about the Candidates and How They Learn It: The 1996 New Hampshire Republican Primary as a Case Study," in Mayer, William, ed., *In Pursuit of the White House 2000* (New York: Chatham House, 2000), 203–54.

Burns, Nancy; Schlozman, Kay; and Verba, Sidney, *The Private Roots of Public Action* (Cambridge, MA: Harvard University Press, 2001).

Busch, Andrew, and Mayer, William, "The Front-Loading Problem," in Mayer, William, ed., *The Making of the Presidential Candidates 2004* (Lanham, MD: Rowman & Littlefield, 2004), 1–44.

Butler, David, and Cain, Bruce, *Congressional Redistricting* (New York: Macmillan, 1992).

Campaign Finance Institute, Press Release, "New Presidential Public Financing Bill: A First Step for Empowering the Voters," 28 July 2006.

___, *So the Voters May Choose*, available for download at http://www.cfinst.org/presidential/report2/index.html.

Campaign Finance Institute Task Force on Presidential Nomination Financing, *Participation, Competition, Engagement: How to Revive and Improve Public Funding for Presidential Nomination Politics* (Washington, DC: Campaign Finance Institute, 2003).

Cappella, Joseph, and Jamieson, Kathleen Hall, *The Spiral of Cynicism* (New York: Oxford University Press, 1997).

Ceaser, James, and Busch, Andrew, *Red Over Blue* (Lanham, MD: Rowman & Littlefield,

2005).

Citrin, Jack, "Comment: The Political Relevance of Trust in Government," *American Political Science Review* 68 (1974): 973–88.

Clymer, Adam, "The 2000 Campaign: The Primaries; G.O.P. Panel Votes to Revise Primary System," *The New York Times,* 3 May 2000, A1.

___, "The 2000 Campaign: The Primaries; G.O.P. Panel Votes to Revise Primary System," *The New York Times*, 13 May 2000, A12.

___, "The 2000 Campaign: The Process; A G.O.P. Overhaul of Primary Season Is Killed by Bush," *The New York Times*, 29 July 2000, A1.

Committee for the Study of the American Electorate, *Two Pro-Participation Reforms Actually Harm Voter Turnout: Other Reforms Suggested* (Washington, DC: Committee for the Study of the American Electorate, 2001).

Common Cause, "Common Cause and Brennan Center File Comments with FEC Regarding 527 Advisory Opinion," Press Release, 17 February 2004, available at http://www.commoncause.org/site/apps/nl/content2.asp?c=dkLNK1MQIwG&b=194883&ct=228115.

___, "Common Cause Submits FEC Comments on 527s," Press Release, 13 April 2004, available at http://www.commoncause.org/site/apps/nl/content2.asp?c=dkLNK1MQIwG&b=194883&ct=228109.

___, "Prospecting for Access: How the Bush Pioneers Shaped Public Policy" (Washington, DC: Common Cause, October 2003), downloaded from www.commoncause.org/just watch.

___, *A Reporter's Guide to Money in Politics: Campaign 2004* (Washington, DC: Common Cause, 25 November 2003).

___, "Statement of Common Cause President Ann McBride at News Conference Asking for Independent Counsel to Investigate Campaign Finance Activities of Clinton, Dole Campaigns," Press Release, 9 October 1996.

Conway, Margaret, *Political Participation in the United States*, 3rd ed. (Washington, DC: CQ Press, 2000).

Cook, Rhodes, *The Presidential Nominating Process, A Place for Us?* (Lanham, MD: Rowman & Littlefield, 2004).

Cornfield, Michael, and Sieger, Jonah, "The Net and the Nomination," in Mayer, William, ed., *The Making of the Presidential Candidates 2004* (Lanham, MD: Rowman & Littlefield, 2004).

Corrado, Anthony, *Campaign Finance Reform: Beyond the Basics* (New York: Century Foundation Press, 2000).

___,"Financing the 2000 Elections," in Pomper, Gerald, ed., *The Election of 2000* (New York: Chatham House, 2001).

___, *Paying for Presidents* (New York: Twentieth Century Fund Press, 1993).

Corrado, Anthony; Barclay, Sarah; and Gouvea, Heitor, "The Parties Take the Lead: Political Parties and the Financing of the 2000 Presidential Election," in Green, John, and Farmer, Rick, eds., *The State of the Parties*, 4th ed. (Lanham, MD: Rowman & Littlefield, 2003).

Corrado, Anthony, and Gouvea, Heitor, "Financing Presidential Nominations under the BCRA," in Mayer, William, ed., *The Making of the Presidential Candidates 2004* (Lanham, MD: Rowman & Littlefield, 2004).

The Correspondents of *The New York Times*, *36 Days: The Complete Chronicle of the 2000 Presidential Election Crisis* (New York: Times Books, 2001).

Cotter, Cornelius; Gibson, James; Bibby, John; and Huckshorn, Robert, *Party Organizations in American Politics* (New York: Praeger, 1984).

Crotty, William, *A Defining Moment* (Armonk, NY: M.E. Sharpe, 2005).

Dalton, Russell, *Citizen Politics*, 4th ed. (Washington, DC: CQ Press, 2006).

Davis, Richard, *Politics Online* (New York: Routledge, 2005).

Democracy 21, "Presidential Funding Act of 2003 Bill Summary," 21 November 2003, available at http://www.democracy21.org/index.asp?Type=B_PR&SEC={FD714569-5FB3-45D6-82D4-A3098EE124BA}&DE={00F9A0CF-5949-4D97-847CA376348353 EA.

Dershowitz, Alan, *Supreme Injustice: How the High Court Hijacked Election 2000* (New York: Oxford University Press, 2001).

DiClerico, Robert and Uslaner, Eric, *Few Are Chosen* (New York: McGraw-Hill Book Company, 1984).

Dionne, E.J., Jr., and Kristol, William, eds., *Bush* v. *Gore: The Court Cases and the Commentary* (Washington, DC: Brookings Institution Press, 2001).

Doppelt, Jack, and Shearer, Ellen, *Non-Voters: America's No Shows* (Thousand Oaks, CA: Sage, 1999).

Dudley, Robert, and Gitelson, Alan, *American Elections: The Rules Matter* (New York: Longman, 2002).

Dulio, David, *For Better or Worse: How Political Consultants Are Changing Elections in the United States* (Albany: State University of New York Press, 2004).

Dulio, David, and Nelson, Candice, *Vital Signs* (Washington, DC: Brookings Institution Press, 2005).

Duncan, Dayton, *Grass Roots: One Year in the Life of the New Hampshire Presidential Primary* (New York: Viking Penguin, 1991).

Eldersveld, Samuel, and Walton, Hanes, Jr., *Political Parties in American Society*, 2nd ed. (Boston: Bedford/St. Martin's, 2000).

FairVote, *Who Picks the President*, a report by FairVote found at www.fairvote.org/presidential.

Fiorina, Morris, *Culture War? The Myth of a Polarized America*, 2nd ed. (New York: Pearson Longman, 2006).

Fowler, Linda; Spiliotes, Constantine; and Vavreck, Linda, "Group Advocacy in the 2000 New Hampshire Primary," in *PS: Political Science and Politics* 34, no. 2, June 2001, 272 for the abstract. The full text is at www.apsanet.org/PS/June01/fowler.cfm.

———, "The Role of Issue Advocacy in the New Hampshire Primary," in Magleby, David, ed., *Getting Inside the Outside Campaign* (Provo, UT: Brigham Young University, Center for the Study of Elections and Democracy, 2000).

Frantzich, Stephen, *Political Parties in the Technological Age* (New York: Longman, 1989).

Galvin, Daniel, "How to Grow a Democratic Majority," *The New York Times*, 3 June 2006, A13.

Gans, Curtis, "Making It Easier Doesn't Work," report available at the Early Voting page of Reformelections.org, http://reformelections.org/feature.asp?menuid={88D32B43-3876-

4B06-A941-25A33211CBE5.

___, "Turnout Exceeds Optimistic Predictions. More Than 122 Million Vote. Highest Turnout in 38 Years," report available at the Early Voting page of Reformelections.org, http://reformelections.org/feature.asp?menuid={88D32B433876-4B06-A94125A33211CBE5.

Gierzynski, Anthony, *Money Rules: Financing Elections in America* (Boulder, CO: Westview Press, 2000).

Gilgoff, Dan, "Dean's List," *U.S. News and World Report*, 24 July 2006.

Green, Donald, and Gerber, Alan, *Get Out the Vote* (Washington, DC: Brookings Institution, 2004).

Green, Donald; Palmquist, Bradley; and Schickler, Eric, *Partisan Hearts and Minds* (New Haven, CT: Yale University Press, 2002).

Green, John, and Bigelow, Nathan, "The 2000 Presidential Nominations: The Costs of Innovation," in Magleby, David, ed., *Financing the 2000 Election* (Washington, DC: Brookings Institution Press, 2002).

Green, John, and Corrado, Anthony, "The Impact of BCRA on Presidential Campaign Finance," in Malbin, Michael, ed., *Life After Reform: When the Bipartisan Campaign Reform Act Meets Politics* (Lanham, MD: Rowman & Littlefield, 2003).

Gregg, Gary, ed., *Securing Democracy: Why We Have an Electoral College* (Boulder, CO: Westview Press, 2001).

Gronke, Paul, *Ballot Integrity and Voting by Mail: The Oregon Experience*, A Report for the Commission on Federal Election Reform, available for download at the website of the Oregon Secretary of State at http://www.sos.state.or.us/executive/policyinitiatives/vbm/execvbm.htm.

Hacker, Andrew, "Does a 'Divisive' Primary Harm a Candidate's Election Chances?," *American Political Science Review* 59 (1965): 105–110.

Hamburger, Tom, and Wallsten, Peter, *One Party Country* (New York: Wiley, 2006).

Hansen, John Mark, "The Majoritarian Influence and the Declining Significance of Place," in Pomper, Gerald, and Weiner, Mark, eds., *The Future of American Democratic Politics* (New Brunswick, NJ: Rutgers University Press, 2003).

Haworth, Paul, *The Hayes-Tilden Disputed Election of 1876* (New York: Russell and Russell, 1966).

Herrnson, Paul, *Congressional Elections: Campaigning at Home and in Washington*, 4th ed. (Washington, DC: CQ Press, 2004).

___, "Reemergent National Party Organizations," in Maisel, L. Sandy, ed., *The Parties Respond* (Boulder, CO: Westview Press, 1990), ch. 3.

Hill, David Lee, *American Voter Turnout: An Institutional Perspective* (Boulder, CO: Westview Press, 2006).

Holder, Kelly, "Voting and Registration in the Election of November 2004," *US Census Bureau*, Report issued March 2006.

Institute for Politics, Democracy and the Internet, *Small Donors and Online Giving* (Washington, DC: The George Washington University Graduate School of Political Management, 2005).

Jacobson, Gary, *A Divider, Not a Uniter: George Bush and the American People* (New York:

Pearson Longman, 2007).

___, *The Politics of Congressional Elections*, 6th ed. (New York: Pearson Longman, 2004).

Johnson, Donald, and Gibson, James, "The Divisive Primary Revisited: Primary Activists in Iowa," *American Political Science Review* 68 (1984): 67–77.

Judas, John, and Teixeria, Rudy, *The Emerging Democratic Majority* (New York: Scribner, 2004).

Justice, Glenn, "The 2004 Campaign: Campaign Finance; F.E.C. Declines to Curb Independent Fund-Raisers," *The New York Times*, 14 May 2004, A18.

___, "The 2004 Campaign: Campaign Finance; Republicans Rush to Form New Finance Groups," *The New York Times*, 29 May 2004, A1.

Karp, Jeffrey, and Banducci, Susan, "Going Postal: How All-Mail Elections Influence Turnout," *Political Behavior* 22 (2000): 223–39.

Keating, Christopher, and Hamilton, Elizabeth, "A Deal at Last," *The Hartford Courant*, 4 May 2006, A1.

Keeter, Scott, "In Search of Ideologues in America: It's Harder Than You May Think," Pew Research Center, 11 April 2006, http://pewresearch.org/obdeck/?ObDeck ID=17.

___, "Politics and the 'DotNet' Generation," Pew Research Center, 30 May 2006.

Keith, Bruce, et al., *The Myth of the Independent Voter* (Berkeley: University of California Press, 1992).

Kellner, Douglas, *Grand Theft 2000: Media Spectacle and a Stolen Election* (Lanham, MD: Rowman & Littlefield, 2001).

Kenney, Patrick, and Rice, Tom, "The Effect of Primary Divisiveness in Gubernatorial and Senatorial Elections," *Journal of Politics* 46 (1984): 904–15.

Kernell, Samuel, *Going Public*, 3rd ed. (Washington, DC: CQ Press, 1997).

Kessel, John, *Presidential Campaign Politics*, 2nd ed. (Homewood, IL: The Dorsey Press, 1984).

Key, V.O., *Politics, Parties and Pressure Groups*, 2nd ed. (New York: Thomas Y. Crowell Co., 1950).

___, *Politics, Parties and Interest Groups*, 5th ed. (New York: Thomas Y. Crowell Co., 1965).

Kirkpatrick, Jeane, *The New Presidential Elite* (New York: Russell Sage, 1976).

Kolodny, Robin, "Electoral Partnerships: Political Consultants and Political Parties," in Thurber, James, and Nelson, Candice, eds., *Campaign Warriors: The Role of Political Consultants in Elections* (Washington, DC: Brookings Institution Press, 2000), ch. 7.

Kolodny, Robin, and Logan, Angela, "Political Consultants and the Extension of Party Goals," *PS: Political Science and Politics* 31 (1998): 155–59.

Kort, Amy, "Estimated Presidential Spending Limits," in The Federal Election Commission, *The Record*, vol. 29, no. 11, November 2003.

Koza, John, et al., *Every Vote Equal* (Los Altos, CA: National Popular Vote Press, 2006).

Kurtz, Howard, "In Advertising Give and Take, Clinton Took and Responded," *The Washington Post*, 6 November 1992, A10.

Lengle, James; Owen, Diana; and Sonner, Molly, "Divisive Nominating Mechanisms and Democratic Party Electoral Prospects," *Journal of Politics* 57 (1995): 370–83.

Lenhart, Amanda, and Fox, Susannah, *Bloggers* (Washington: The Pew Internet and American

Life Project), 19 July 2006.

Lijphart, Arend, "Compulsory Voting Is the Best Way to Keep Democracy Strong," *Chronicle of Higher Education*, 18 October 1996, B3–4.

Lipset, Seymour Martin, and Schneider, William, *The Confidence Gap* (Baltimore: Johns Hopkins University Press, 1987).

___, "The Confidence Gap During the Reagan Years, 1981–1987," *Political Science Quarterly* 102 (1987): 1–23.

Longley, Lawrence, and Peirce, Neal, *The Electoral College Primer 2000* (New Haven, CT: Yale University Press, 1999).

Macedo, Stephen, et al., *Democracy at Risk* (Washington, DC: Brookings Institution Press, 2005).

Madison, James, "Letter to George Hay," 23 August 1823, printed in Farrand, Max, ed., *The Records of the Federal Constitutional Convention of 1787*, vol. 3 (New Haven, CT: Yale University Press, 1937).

Magleby, David, ed., *Financing the 2000 Election* (Washington, DC: Brookings Institution Press, 2002).

___, ed., *Getting Inside the Outside Campaign* (Provo, UT: Brigham Young University, Center for the Study of Elections and Democracy, 2000).

Magleby, David, and Monson, Quin, eds., *The Last Hurrah* (Provo, UT: Brigham Young University, Center for the Study of Elections and Democracy, 2003).

Magleby, David; Monson, Quin; and Patterson, Kelly, eds., *Dancing Without Partners* (Lanham, MD: Rowman & Littlefield, 2006).

___, eds., *dancing without partners* (Provo, UT: Brigham Young University, Center for the Study of Elections and Democracy, 2005).

Maisel, L. Sandy, *Parties and Elections in America*, 2nd ed. (New York: McGraw-Hill, 1993).

Malbin, Michael, ed., *The Election After Reform* (Lanham, MD: Rowman & Littlefield, 2006).

___, ed., *Life After Reform: When the Bipartisan Campaign Reform Act Meets Politics* (Lanham, MD: Rowman & Littlefield, 2003).

Mann, Thomas, and Ornstein, Norman, "Separating Myth from Reality in McConnell v. FEC," *Election Law Journal*, March 2002.

Mathews, David, *Politics for People: Finding a Responsible Voice* (Urbana: University of Illinois Press, 1994).

Mayer, Kenneth; Werner, Timothy; and Williams, Amanda, "Do Public Funding Programs Enhance Electoral Competition?," updated version, March 2005, 6, available at the website of the Wisconsin Campaign Finance Project, http://campfin.polisci.wisc.edu/.

Mayer, William, "Mass Partisanship," in Shafer, Byron, ed., *Partisan Approaches to Postwar American Politics* (New York: Chatham House, 1998), ch. 5.

___, ed., *In Pursuit of the White House 2000* (New York: Chatham House, 2000).

___, ed., *The Making of the Presidential Candidates 2004* (Lanham, MD: Rowman & Littlefield, 2004).

Mayer, William, and Busch, Andrew, *The Front-Loading Problem in Presidential Nominations* (Washington, DC: Brookings Institution, 2004).

McDonald, Michael, "Up, Up and Away! Voter Participation in the 2004 Presidential Election," *The Forum* 2:4 (2004), article 4, at http://www.bepress.com/forum/vol2/iss4/art4.

McDonald, Michael, and Popkin, Samuel, "The Myth of the Vanishing Voter," *American Political Science Review* 95 (2001): 963–74.

Menfee-Libey, David, *The Triumph of Campaign-Centered Politics* (New York: Chatham House, 2000).

Miller, Arthur, "Political Issues and Trust in Government: 1964–1970," *American Political Science Review* 68 (1974): 951–72.

Miller, Warren, and Jennings, Kent, *Parties in Transition: A Longitudinal Study of Party Elites and Supporters* (New York: Russell Sage Foundation, 1988).

Mueller, John, *War, Presidents and Public Opinion* (New York: John Wiley and Sons, 1973).

Nagourney, Adam, "Candidates Face Sprawling and Complex Electoral Map," *The New York Times*, 12 May 2004, A18.

___, "Dean and Party Leaders in a Money Dispute," *The New York Times*, 11 May 2006, A31.

___, "Democrats Hear From 8 Who Want to Lead Party," *The New York Times*, 12 December 2004, 1:44.

___, "Democrats Propose Moving Up Nevada in Presidential Caucuses," *The New York Times*, 23 July 2006, A1.

___, "Internet Injects Sweeping Change into U.S. Politics," *The New York Times*, 2 April 2006, 1:1.

National Annenberg Election Survey, "Early Voting Reaches Record Levels in 2004, National Annenberg Election Survey Shows," Press Release, 24 March 2005.

Nelson, Michael, *The Elections of 2004* (Washington, DC: CQ Press, 2005).

Niemi, Richard, and Junn, Jane, *Civic Education: What Makes Students Learn* (New Haven, CT: Yale University Press, 1998).

Nixon, Richard, *Six Crises* (Garden City, NY: Doubleday, 1962).

Norris, Pippa, *Count Every Voice: Democratic Participation Worldwide* (New York: Cambridge University Press, 2002).

Oliver, J. Eric, "The Effect of Eligibility Restrictions and Party Activity on Absentee Voting and Overall Turnout," *American Journal of Political Science* 40 (1996): 498–513.

Ono, Keiko, "Electoral Origins of Partisan Polarization in Congress: Debunking the Myth," *Extensions, A Journal of the Carl Albert Congressional Research and Studies Center* (Fall 2005): 15–19, 25.

Palmer, Niall, *The New Hampshire Primary and the American Electoral Process* (Westport, CT: Praeger, 1997).

Patterson, Thomas, *The Vanishing Voter* (New York: Alfred A. Knopf, 2002).

Pazniakos, Mark, "Campaign Finance Reform Becomes Law," *The Hartford Courant*, 8 December 2005, B8.

Pazniakos, Mark, and Keating, Christopher, "Senate Passes Reform Package," *The Hartford Courant*, 1 December 2005, A1.

Peirce, Neal, and Longley, Lawrence, *The People's President: The Electoral College in American History and the Direct Vote Alternative*, rev. ed. (New Haven, CT: Yale University Press, 1981).

Pew Research Center for the People and the Press, "Americans' Support for Israel Unchanged by Recent Hostilities," 26 July 2006.

___, "Dubai Ports Fallout: Bush Approval Falls to 33%, Congress Earns Rare Praise," 15

March 2006.

___, *Mapping the Political Landscape 2005* (Washington, DC: The Pew Research Center, 2005).

___, *Maturing Internet News Audience—Broader Than Deep; Online Papers Modestly Boost Newspaper Readership*, 30 July 2006.

___, *Online News Audience Larger, More Diverse. News Audience Increasingly Politicized*, 8 June 2004.

___, "Public Disillusionment with Congress at Record Levels," 20 April 2006.

___, "Public Sours on Government and Business," 25 October 2005.

Piven, Frances Fox, and Cloward, Richard, *Why Americans Don't Vote* (New York: Pantheon Books, 1988).

Polsby, Nelson, *Consequences of Party Reform* (New York: Oxford University Press, 1983).

Polsby, Nelson, and Wildavsky, Aaron, *Presidential Elections*, 10th ed. (New York: Chatham House, 2000).

Pomper, Gerald, ed., *The Election of 2000* (New York: Chatham House, 2001).

___, "The Presidential Election," in Nelson, Michael, *The Elections of 2004* (Washington, DC: CQ Press, 2005).

Posner, Richard, *Breaking the Deadlock: The 2000 Election, the Constitution and the Courts* (Princeton, NJ: Princeton University Press, 2001).

Putnam, Robert, *Democracies in Flux: The Evolution of Social Capital in Contemporary Society* (Oxford: Oxford University Press, 2002).

___, "Bowling Together," *American Prospect*, 12 February 2002, 20–22.

___, *Bowling Alone: The Collapse and Renewal of American Community* (New York: Simon and Schuster, 2000).

___, "The Strange Disappearance of Civic America," *American Prospect* 24 (Winter 1996): 34–48.

___, "Bowling Alone," *Journal of Democracy* 6 (1995): 65–78.

Ranney, Austin, *Curing the Mischiefs of Faction: Party Reform in America* (Berkeley: University of California Press, 1975).

Redlawsk, David, and Sanders, Arthur, "The Iowa Senate and 1st, 2nd, 3rd, and 4th Congressional District Races," in Magleby, David, and Monson, Quin, eds., *The Last Hurrah* (Provo, UT: Brigham Young University, Center for the Study of Elections and Democracy, 2003), ch. 3.

___,"The 2002 Iowa House and Senate Elections: The More Things Change…" *PS* 36 (July 2003): 406, (abstract) and at www.apsanet.org/PS/july03/redlawsk.pdf (article).

___, "Groups and the Grassroots in the Iowa Caucuses," in *PS: Political Science and Politics* 34, no. 2, June 2001, 270 for the abstract; full text is at www.apsanet.org/PS/June01 /redlawsk.cfm.

Reid, T.R., "Most Americans Feel They're on Sidelines of Political Process, Poll Finds," *The Washington Post*, 18 March 2004, A6.

Robinson, Michael, and Sheehan, Margaret, *Over the Wire and on TV: CBS and UPI in Campaign '80* (New York: Russell Sage Foundation, 1983).

Roche, John, "The Founding Fathers: A Reform Caucus in Action," *American Political Science Review* 55 (December 1961): 799-816.

Rosenstone, Steven, and Hansen, John Mark, *Mobilization, Participation and Democracy in America* (New York: Longman, 2003).

Rutenberg, Jim, "The 2004 Campaign; First Debate Draws Large TV Audience," *The New York Times,* 2 October 2004, A10.

___, "The 2004 Campaign: Shaping Reactions," *The New York Times*, 4 October 2004, A1.

Sabato, Larry, *The Rise of Political Consultants: New Ways of Winning Elections* (New York: Basic Books, 1981).

___, ed., *Overtime: The Election 2000 Thriller* (New York: Longman Publishers, 2002).

Sanders, Arthur, "The Impact of BCRA on the Presidential Nomination Process: The 2004 Iowa Caucuses," in Magleby, David; Monson, Quin; and Patterson, Kelly, eds., *Dancing Without Partners* (Lanham, MD: Rowman & Littlefield, 2006), ch. 3.

___, "Taking It to the Streets: The Iowa Presidential Campaign of 2004," in Magleby, David; Monson, Quin; and Patterson, Kelly, eds., *Dancing Without Partners* (Lanham, MD: Rowman & Littlefield, 2006), ch. 4.

Sanders, Arthur, and Redlawsk, David, "Money and the Iowa Caucuses," in Magleby, David, ed., *Getting Inside the Outside Campaign* (Provo, UT: Brigham Young University, Center for the Study of Elections and Democracy, 2000).

Schumaker, Paul, and Loomis, Burdett, eds., *Choosing a President: The Electoral College and Beyond* (Chatham, NJ: Chatham House, 2002).

Seelye, Katharine, "How to Sell a Candidate to a Porsche-Driving, Leno-Loving Nascar Fan," *The New York Times*, 6 December 2004, A16.

The Sentencing Project, "Felony Disenfranchisement Laws in the United States," http://www.sentencingproject.org/pubs_05.cfm.

Shafer, Byron, *Bifurcated Politics* (Cambridge, MA: Harvard University Press, 1988).

___, ed., *Partisan Approaches to Postwar American Politics* (New York: Chatham House, 1998).

___, "Partisan Elites: 1946–1996," ch. 3 of Shafer, Byron, ed., *Partisan Approaches to Postwar American Politics* (New York: Chatham House, 1998).

___, ed., *Postwar Politics in the G-7: Orders and Eras in Comparative Perspective* (Madison: University of Wisconsin Press, 1996).

___, *Quiet Revolution: The Struggle for the Democratic Party and the Shaping of Post-Reform Politics* (New York: Russell Sage Foundation, 1983).

Simon, Don, *McConnell v. FEC: BCRA Analysis*, 12 December 2003, found at www.commoncause.org/news/default.cfm?ArtID=261.

___, *McConnell v. FEC*, an Analysis of the Case in an Open Letter to the Common Cause Community, 11 December 2003, available for download as a PDF at www.commoncause.org/atf/cf/%7BFB3C17E2CDD14DF692BEBD4429893665%7D/DJS-Supreme%20Court%20Analysis.pdf.

Skocpol, Theda, *Diminished Democracy* (Norman: University of Oklahoma Press, 2003).

Skocpol, Theda, and Fiorina, Morris, eds., *Civic Engagement in American Democracy* (Washington, DC: Brookings Institution, 1999).

Sorauf, Frank, *Money in American Elections* (Glenview, IL: Scott Foresman, 1988).

Southwell, Priscella, "Five Years Later: A Re-Assessment of Oregon's Vote by Mail Electoral Process," available for download at the website of the Oregon Secretary of State at http://www.sos.state.or.us/executive/policy-initiatives/vbm/execvbm.htm.

"Stamp of Approval?," *The Economist*, 16 March 2006.

Stanley, Alessandra, "The 2004 Campaign: On Television: Bush Smiles, but Laughter Falls Short," *The New York Times*, 14 October 2004, A18.

Stone, Walter, "The Carryover Effect in Presidential Elections," *American Political Science Review* 80 (1986): 271–80.

Stonecash, Jeffrey, *Class and Party in American Politics* (Boulder, CO: Westview Press, 2000).

___, *Political Parties Matter: Realignment and the Return of Partisan Voting* (Boulder, CO: Lynne Rienner Publishers, 2006).

A Study of Political Strategy and Tactics (Washington, DC: The American Institute for Political Communication, 1967).

Sunstein, Cass, *republic.com* (Princeton, NJ: Princeton University Press, 2001).

Tapper, Jake, *Down and Dirty: The Plot to Steal the Presidency* (New York: Little Brown, 2001).

Teixeira, Rudy, *The Disappearing American Voter* (Washington, DC: Brookings Institution, 1992).

Theiss-Smith, Elizabeth, and Braunstein, Richard, "The Nationalization of Local Politics in South Dakota," in Magleby, David; Monson, Quin; and Patterson, Kelly, eds., *Dancing Without Partners* (Provo, UT: Brigham Young University, Center for the Study of Elections and Democracy, 2005).

Tolchin, Susan, *The Angry American*, 2nd ed. (Boulder, CO: Westview Press, 1989).

Valelly, Richard, *The Two Reconstructions* (Chicago: University of Chicago Press, 2004).

Verba, Sidney, and Nie, Norman, *Participation in America* (New York: Harper & Row, 1972).

Verba, Sidney; Nie, Norman; and Kim, Jae-On, *Participation and Political Equality* (Cambridge: Cambridge University Press, 1978).

Verba, Sidney; Schlozman, Kay; and Brady, Henry, *Voice and Equality* (Cambridge, MA: Harvard University Press, 1995).

Ware, Alan, *The American Direct Primary* (New York: Cambridge University Press, 2002).

The Washington State Association of County Auditors, "Mail Voting in the Stadium Election," 28 July 1997, available for download at the website of the Oregon Secretary of State at http://www.sos.state.or.us/executive/policy-initiatives /vbm/execvbm.htm.

Wattenberg, Martin, *The Decline of American Political Parties, 1952–1994* (Cambridge, MA: Harvard University Press, 1996).

___, *Is Voting for Young People* (New York: Pearson Longman, 2007).

___, *Where Have All the Voters Gone* (Cambridge, MA: Harvard University Press, 2002).

Wayne, Steven, *Is This Any Way to Run a Democratic Election* (Boston: Houghton Mifflin, 2001).

___, *The Road to the White House 2000* (New York: Bedford/St. Martin's, 2000).

___, *The Road to the White House 2004* (Belmont, CA: Thomson Wadsworth, 2004).

Weissman, Steve, "CFI Analysis of the Presidential Candidates' Financial Reports Filed April 20: Bush and Kerry Emphasized Small Contributions," Campaign Finance Institute Press Release, 22 April 2004, available at www.cfinst.org/pr/042202.html.

___, "CFI Analysis of Presidential Candidates' Financial Reports Filed June 20," Campaign Finance Institute Press Release, 30 June 2004, available at http://www.cfinst.org/pr/063004.html.

___, "CFI Analysis of the Presidential Candidates' Financial Reports Filed August 20, 2004," Campaign Finance Institute Press Release, 25 August 2004, available at http://www.cfinst.org/pr/082504.html.

Weissman, Stephen, and Hassan, Ruth, "BCRA and the 527 Groups," in Malbin, Michael, ed., *The Election After Reform* (Lanham, MD: Rowman & Littlefield, 2006).

Weissman, Stephen, and Ryan, Kara, "Non-Profit Interest Groups' Election Activities and Federal Campaign Finance Policy" (Washington, DC: The Campaign Finance Institute, July 2006).

Wertheimer, Fred, "FEC Rulemaking Proceeding Will Determine Whether FEC Recreates Soft Money System in the 2004 Federal Elections," A Report for Democracy 21, 19 February 2004, available at http://www.democracy21.org/index.asp?Type=B_PR&SEC={7248831A-87CA-4C2DB87360C64918C920}&DE={4D4D2E91-2A1F4DB7-A3E3-E9668567E601}.

West, Darrell, *Air Wars*, 3rd ed. (Washington, DC: CQ Press, 2001).

West, Darrell; Kern, Montague; Alger, Dean; and Goggin, Janice, "Ad Buys in Presidential Campaigns," *Political Communications* 12 (1995): 275–90.

White, John Kenneth, and Shea, Daniel, *New Party Politics: From Jefferson and Hamilton to the Information Age*, 2nd ed. (Belmont, CA: Thompson/Wadsworth, 2004).

White, Theodore, *The Making of the President 1960* (New York: Pocket Books, 1961).

Wilcox, Clyde, *Onward Christian Soldiers: The Religious Right in American Politics* (Boulder, CO: Westview Press, 1996).

Wilenz, Sean, *The Rise of American Democracy: Jefferson to Lincoln* (New York: W.W. Norton, 2005).

Wilson, James Q., *The Amateur Democrat* (Chicago: University of Chicago Press, 1966).

Winebrenner, Hugh, *The Iowa Precinct Caucuses: The Making of a Media Event*, 2nd ed. (Ames: Iowa State University Press, 1998).

Wolfinger, Raymond, and Rosenstone, Steven, *Who Votes* (New Haven, CT: Yale University Press, 1980).

The World Watch Institute, "Matters of Scale—Advertising War for a War President," at www.worldwatch.org/node/802.

Zelany, Jeff, "A Third in Iowa Poll Meet, Hear Candidates," *Des Moines Register*, 10 January 2000, A1.

Zelnick, Robert, *Winning Florida: How the Bush Team Fought the Battle* (Stanford, CA: Hoover Institution Press, 2001).

Zukin, Cliff, et al., *A New Engagement? Political Participation, Civic Life, and the Changing American Citizen* (New York: Oxford University Press, 2006.

INDEX

Popular Politics
& Governance
In America

Steven E. Schier, General Editor

Popular Politics and Governance in America, a new series of books on contemporary political science, seeks to publish scholarly and teaching materials about the processes of popular politics and the operations of governmental institutions at both the national and state levels. Although many titles in this series will appeal to graduate and professional audiences, they will employ qualitative and quantitative analysis in fashions primarily appropriate for undergraduate classrooms. Topics will include studies of parties, interest groups, elections, public opinion, chief executives, legislatures, and the bureaucracy. Peter Lang views this new series as a flagship among their several on-going series that have published numerous well-received and useful volumes in political science.

For additional information about this series or for the submission of manuscripts, please contact:

Peter Lang Publishing, Inc.
29 Broadway, 18th floor
New York, New York 10006

To order other books in this series, please contact our Customer Service Department:

(800) 770-LANG (within the U.S.)
(212) 647-7706 (outside the U.S.)
(212) 647-7707 FAX

Or browse online by series:

www.peterlang.com